CONTENTS

Chapter One: Depression

Depression	1
Terms you might hear	4
Depression and physical illness	5
Are you at risk for depression?	6
Depression is UK's biggest social problem	7
Teenage depression	8
Depression and underage drinking	9
Ecstasy and depression	10
Depression and suicide	10
New reports link mental ill-health to changing diets	11
Men and depression	13
Statistics on mental health	16
Post-natal depression	17
Feeling SAD?	18
Manic depression	19
Myths and misconceptions about depression	21
Depression in the elderly	22

Chapter Two: Treating Depression

Treating depression	24
Pills 'are not best way to treat child depression'	27
Tips on depression and anxiety in children	28
Introduction to talking therapies	29
End of the 'prozac nation'	30
Quick guide to antidepressants	32
Psychotherapy for all?	33
Electroconvulsive therapy	34
Responding to depression	35
Cheers?	36
The lowdown: seasonal affective disorder (SAD)	37
Quick-fix tips for depression	39
Key Facts	40
Glossary	41
Index	42
Additional Resources	43
Acknowledgements	44

00089210690010

Introduction

Understanding Depression is the one hundred and twenty fifth volume in the **Issues** series. The aim of this series is to offer up-to-date information about important issues in our world.

Understanding Depression looks at the issue of depression and mental ill-health, as well as the different kinds of treatments used for depression.

The information comes from a wide variety of sources and includes:
Government reports and statistics
Newspaper reports and features
Magazine articles and surveys
Website material
Literature from lobby groups
and charitable organisations.

It is hoped that, as you read about the many aspects of the issues explored in this book, you will critically evaluate the information presented. It is important that you decide whether you are being presented with facts or opinions. Does the writer give a biased or an unbiased report? If an opinion is being expressed, do you agree with the writer?

Understanding Depression offers a useful starting-point for those who need convenient access to information about the many issues involved. However, it is only a starting-point. Following each article is a URL to the relevant organisation's website, which you may wish to visit for further information.

*****

Understanding Depression

ISSUES

Volume 125

Series Editor

Craig Donnellan

Assistant Editor

Lisa Firth

Independence

Educational Publishers
Cambridge

First published by Independence
PO Box 295
Cambridge CB1 3XP
England

British Library Cataloguing in Publication Data
Understanding Depression – (Issues Series)
I. Donnellan, Craig II. Series
616.8'527

ISBN 1 86168 364 2

Printed in Great Britain
MWL Print Group Ltd

Layout by
Lisa Firth

Cover
The illustration on the front cover is by
Simon Kneebone.

Depression

Information from the Royal College of Psychiatrists

his information is for anyone who is troubled by feelings of depression. We hope it will also be useful for the friends and relatives of anyone who is feeling like this.

It describes what it feels like to be depressed, how you can help yourself, how to help someone else who is depressed, and what help you can get from professionals. It mentions some of the things we don't know about depression. At the end of the leaflet there is a list of other places where you can get further information.

The feeling of depression is much more powerful and unpleasant than the short episodes of unhappiness that we all experience from time to time

---

Introduction

We all feel fed up, miserable or sad at times. These feelings don't usually last longer than a week or two, and they don't interfere too much with our lives. Sometimes there's a reason, sometimes they just come out of the blue. We usually cope with them ourselves. We may have a chat with a friend but don't otherwise need any help. Someone is said to be significantly depressed, or suffering from depression, when:

- their feelings of depression don't go away quickly; and
- they are so bad that they interfere with their everyday life.

What does it feel like to be depressed?

The feeling of depression is much more powerful and unpleasant than

the short episodes of unhappiness that we all experience from time to time. It goes on for much longer. It can last for months rather than days or weeks. Most people with depression will not have all the symptoms listed here, but most will have at least five or six.

You:

- feel unhappy most of the time (but may feel a little better in the evenings);
- lose interest in life and can't enjoy anything;
- find it harder to make decisions;
- can't cope with things that you used to;
- feel utterly tired;
- feel restless and agitated;

- lose appetite and weight (some people find they do the reverse and put on weight);
- take one to two hours to get off to sleep, and then wake up earlier than usual;
- lose interest in sex;
- lose your self-confidence;
- feel useless, inadequate and hopeless;
- avoid other people;
- feel irritable;
- feel worse at a particular time each day, usually in the morning;
- think of suicide.

We may not realise how depressed we are, because it has come on so gradually. We may be determined to struggle on and can blame ourselves for being lazy or feeble. Other people may need to persuade us that it is not a sign of weakness to seek help.

We may try to cope with our feelings of depression by being very busy. This can make us even more stressed and exhausted. We will often notice physical pains, constant headaches or sleeplessness.

Sometimes these physical symptoms can be the first sign of a depression.

Why does it happen?

As in the everyday depression that we all experience from time to time, there will sometimes be an obvious reason for becoming depressed, sometimes not. There is usually more than one reason, and these are different for different people.

The reason may seem obvious. It can be a disappointment, frustration, losing something or someone important. Sometimes it isn't clear why we feel depressed. We're just 'in a mood', 'have got the hump', 'feel blue', 'got out of bed the wrong side'. We really don't know why. Either way, these feelings can become so bad that we need help.

Things that happen in our lives

It is normal to feel depressed after a distressing event, such as bereavement, a divorce or losing a job. We may spend time over the next few weeks or months thinking and talking about it. After a while we seem to come to terms with what's happened. But some of us get stuck in a depressed mood, which doesn't seem to lift.

Circumstances

If we are alone, have no friends around, are stressed, have other worries or are physically run down, we are more likely to become depressed.

Physical illness

Depression often strikes when we are physically ill. This is true for life-threatening illnesses such as cancer and heart disease, but also for illnesses that are long and uncomfortable or painful, like arthritis or bronchitis. Younger people may become depressed after viral infections, like 'flu' or glandular fever.

It can seem to other people that a person with depression has just 'given in', as if they have a choice in the matter

---

Personality

Anyone can become depressed, but some of us seem to be more likely to than others. This may be because of the particular make-up of our body, because of experiences early in our life, or both.

Alcohol

Many people who drink too much alcohol become depressed. It often isn't clear as to which came first – the drinking or the depression. We know that people who drink too much are more likely to kill themselves than other people.

Gender

Women seem to get depressed more than men do. This is possibly because men are less likely to admit their feelings, bottle them up or express them in aggression or through drinking heavily. Women may be more likely to have the double stress of having to work and, at the same time, look after children.

Genes

Depression can run in families. If you have one parent who has become severely depressed, then you are about eight times more likely to become depressed yourself.

What about manic depression?

About one in 10 people who suffer from serious depression will also have periods when they are elated and overactive. This used to be called manic depression, but is now often called bipolar affective disorder. It affects the same number of men and women and tends to run in families.

Isn't depression just a form of weakness?

It can seem to other people that a person with depression has just 'given in', as if they have a choice in the matter. The fact is, there comes a point at which depression is much more like an illness than anything else. It can happen to the most determined of people, and calls for help, not criticism. It is not a sign of weakness – even powerful personalities can experience deep depression. Winston Churchill called it his 'black dog'.

When should I seek help

- When your feelings of depression are worse than usual, and don't seem to get any better.
- When your feelings of depression affect your work, interests and feelings towards your family and friends.
- If you find yourself feeling that life is not worth living, or that

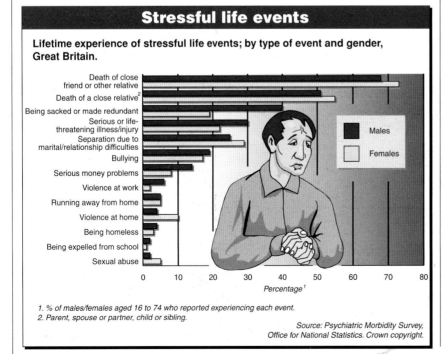

Stressful life events

Lifetime experience of stressful life events; by type of event and gender, Great Britain.

Death of close friend or other relative
Death of a close relative[2]
Being sacked or made redundant
Serious or life-threatening illness/injury
Separation due to marital/relationship difficulties
Bullying
Serious money problems
Violence at work
Running away from home
Violence at home
Being homeless
Being expelled from school
Sexual abuse

Males
Females

0 10 20 30 40 50 60 70 80
Percentage[1]

1. % of males/females aged 16 to 74 who reported experiencing each event.
2. Parent, spouse or partner, child or sibling.

Source: Psychiatric Morbidity Survey, Office for National Statistics. Crown copyright.

other people would be better off without you.

It may be enough to talk things over with a relative or friend, who may be able to help you through a bad patch in your life. If this doesn't seem to help, you probably need to talk it over with your family doctor. You may find that your friends and family notice a difference in you and are worried about you.

Helping yourself

1. Don't keep it to yourself

If you've had some bad news, or a major upset, try to tell someone close to you, and tell them how you feel. It often helps to go over the painful experience several times, to cry about it, and to talk things over with someone. This is part of the mind's natural way of healing.

About one in 10 people who suffer from serious depression will also have periods when they are elated and overactive. This used to be called manic depression, but is now often called bipolar affective disorder

---

2. Do something

Get out of doors for some exercise, even if only for a walk. This will help you to keep physically fit, and you

may sleep better. You may not feel able to work, but it is always good to try to keep active. This could be housework, do-it-yourself (even as little as changing a light bulb) or any part of your normal routine. It can help take your mind off painful thoughts which make you more depressed.

3. Eat well

Try to eat a good, balanced diet, even though you may not feel like eating. Fresh fruit and vegetables are particularly good. Depression can make you lose weight and run short of vitamins, which only makes matters worse.

4. Beware alcohol!

Resist the temptation to drown your sorrows with a drink. Alcohol actually makes depression worse. It may make you feel better for a few hours, but will then make you feel worse again. Too much alcohol stops you from seeking the right help and

from solving problems; it is also bad for your physical health.

5. Sleep

Try not to worry about finding it difficult to sleep. It can be helpful to listen to the radio or watch TV while you're lying down and resting your body, even if you can't sleep. If you can occupy your mind in this way, you may feel less anxious and find it easier to get off to sleep.

6. Tackle the cause

If you think you know what is behind your depression, it can help to write down the problem and then think of the things you could do to tackle it. Pick the best things to do and try them.

7. Keep hopeful

Remind yourself that:

■ you are suffering from an experience which many other people have gone through;

■ you will eventually come out of it, although you may find it hard to believe at the time;

■ depression can be a useful experience – you may come out of it stronger and better able to cope. It can help you to see situations and relationships more clearly;

■ you may be able to make important decisions and changes in your life, which you were avoiding before.

■ The above information is an extract from the Royal College of Psychiatrists' factsheet 'Depression' and is reprinted with permission. Visit www.rcpsych.ac.uk for more information.

© *Royal College of Psychiatrists*

Terms you might hear

Everyone's experience of depression is different. However, several specific types of depression have been identified

Reactive depression

This type of depression is triggered by a traumatic, difficult or stressful event, and people affected will feel low, anxious, irritable, even angry. Reactive depression can also follow prolonged period of stress and can begin even after the stress is over.

Endogenous depression

Endogenous depression is not always triggered by an upsetting or stressful event. Those affected by this common form of depression will experience physical symptoms such as weight change, tiredness, sleeping problems and low mood, as well as poor concentration and low self-esteem.

Seasonal Affective Disorder (SAD) generally coincides with the approach of winter. It is often linked to shortening of daylight hours and lack of sunlight

Manic depression (also known as bipolar depression)

People with manic depression experience mood swings, with 'highs' of excessive energy and elation, to 'lows' of utter despair and lethargy. Delusions or hallucinations can also occur. Most people with this condition have their first episode in their late teens or early twenties. Visit the Manic Depression Fellowship for more information.

Seasonal affective disorder (SAD)

This type of depression generally coincides with the approach of winter. It is often linked to shortening of daylight hours and lack of sunlight.

DepressionAlliance

Symptoms will include wanting to sleep excessively and cravings for carbohydrates or sweet foods. Special 'light boxes' can be used to treat this kind of depression.

Post-natal depression

Many new mothers will experience baby blues; mood swings, crying spells and feelings of loneliness three or four days after giving birth. Post-natal depression will, however, last for much longer and will include symptoms such as panic attacks, sleeping difficulties, having overwhelming fears about dying, and feelings of inadequacy and being unable to cope.

Post-natal depression is a common condition, affecting between 10% and 20% of new mothers. Starting two or three weeks after delivery, it often develops slowly, making it more difficult to diagnose. Often it goes unrecognised by the woman herself,

---

People with manic depression experience mood swings, with 'highs' of excessive energy and elation, to 'lows' of utter despair and lethargy

---

or by her family. For more information about post-natal depression, visit the publications page of the Depression Alliance website to download a free leaflet or go to community links for a list of organisations.

■ The above information is reprinted with kind permission from the Depression Alliance. Visit www.depressionalliance.org for more information.

© Depression Alliance

Prevalence of neurotic disorders

Prevalence of neurotic disorder among adults[1] by sex, 2000, Great Britain.

Disorder	Females	Males
Panic disorder	0.7%	0.7%
All phobias	2.2%	1.3%
Obsessive compulsive disorder	1.3%	0.9%
Depressive episode	2.8%	2.3%
Generalised anxiety disorder	4.6%	4.3%
Mixed anxiety and depressive disorder	10.8%	6.8%
Any neurotic disorder[2]	19.4%	13.5%

Percentage

1. Those aged 16 to 74 years living in private households in Great Britain.
2. People may have more than one type of neurotic disorder so the percentage disorder is not the sum of those with specific disorders.

Source: Psychiatric Morbidity Survey, Office for National Statistics. Crown copyright.

Depression and physical illness

Written by Dr Alan Thomas, lecturer and honorary specialist registrar in psychiatry

Mood changes and depressive illnesses are more common in people suffering from physical illnesses than in people who are well. Although a person can develop depression in association with almost any physical illness, some diseases are more likely to lead to depression than others. Depression in these conditions can be expected to respond to the same treatments (medication and psychosocial treatments) as any other depressive illness, and so help should be sought and treatment given for the depression, irrespective of its cause.

Some physical illnesses, particularly heart disease and other conditions that affect the blood supply, are more likely to occur in people with depression. It is not simply that physical illnesses can lead to depression – the opposite occurs too. This makes the recognition and treatment of depression all the more urgent.

Physical illnesses in which depression is common

Below are some of the more common conditions in which depression is likely to occur.

Diseases of the nervous system

- Parkinson's disease: about 40 per cent of those with Parkinson's disease will suffer from an episode of depression. It is often missed because some of the symptoms of Parkinson's disease are similar to those of depression. For example, slow movements and reduced speech occur in both depression and Parkinson's disease. It seems likely that the increased occurrence of depression in Parkinson's disease results from both the direct effects of the disease on the brain and the impact of the condition on the sufferer's everyday life.

- Dementia: people with dementia suffer from more depressive symptoms and more depressive illnesses than other people. The difficulty these people have in communicating their distress means the depression can be missed and not treated. The development of features such as a loss of interaction and interest in others and a sense of gloominess may mean that a depressive illness is developing and help should be sought.

- Multiple sclerosis: depression is more common in this condition, too. It is not clear how much of the depression arises from the effects of the disease on the brain and how much results through the consequences of the disability.

Vascular diseases (diseases of the blood vessels)

- Heart disease: depression is more common in people with heart disease. It is increased in those suffering from angina (chest pain triggered by thickening of the arteries), and is two to three times more common in people after a heart attack (your doctor may refer to this as a myocardial infarction or MI). Depression in such circumstances also leads to problems for people recovering from a heart attack, making them more at risk of another heart attack. In addition, they may have more difficulty returning to work and more general disability.

- Stroke (cerebrovascular accident): similarly, depression is much more common in people after a stroke and is probably increased in people having 'ministrokes' too (your doctor may refer to these as transient ischaemic attacks or TIAs). Again, those who suffer depression tend to have a more severe and prolonged illness than those with no depression.

- Hypertension (high blood pressure): studies have shown this also leads to increased rates of depression.

Endocrine disorders

- Hypothyroidism (decreased metabolism): low levels of thyroid hormones can lead to depression, which may be very severe. However, unlike the conditions mentioned above, treatment of the hypothyroidism itself (with thyroxine to replace the missing hormone) can also treat the depression.

Some physical illnesses, particularly conditions that affect the blood supply, are more likely to occur in people with depression

---

- Cushing's syndrome: this is a rare disease caused by an excess of certain steroid hormones that can lead to severe depression. Like hypothyroidism, treatment of the underlying physical illness can be very effective in helping to treat the depression too.

Infections

- Certain viral infections, for example glandular fever (infectious mononucleosis) and influenza (flu), are prone to trigger depression in vulnerable individuals.

Prescribed medication

- Certain types of medication are associated with increased rates of depression, for example calcium channel blockers (e.g. nifedipine, nimodipine, verapamil), beta-blockers (e.g. propranolol, atenolol, metoprolol), corticosteroids (e.g. dexamethasone, hydrocortisone) and levodopa (e.g. madopar, sinemet). If depressive symptoms develop after taking a new medicine, then advice should be sought from a doctor about whether to try an alternative.

How do you recognise depression in such physical illnesses?

It is important to be aware of the possibility of depression, especially when a person is suffering from one of illnesses mentioned. The difficulty is that some of the key symptoms in depression are very common in these conditions, e.g. disturbed sleep, poor appetite and tiredness.

This makes these symptoms less helpful for doctors when making the diagnosis of depression. Furthermore, sadness is common following diagnosis of an illness as the sufferer comes to terms with their condition, but a prolonged 'low' mood with frequent weeping is likely to indicate depression has developed.

A physically ill person displaying the following symptoms may in fact be depressed.

- Persistent sadness that does not lift with happy experiences;
- Lack of interest in activities and pastimes that are normally enjoyed;
- Loss of interest in sex;
- A loss of interest in friends and socialising;
- Feelings of guilt and self-blame.
- Marked pessimism about the future;
- Suicidal thoughts and talk of wishing one were dead.

What causes depression in people with physical illnesses?

Just as the cause or causes of depression in people with no physical illness are often not clear, so it is with those who also have a physical illness.

There is good evidence that some of the above illnesses directly affect the parts of the brain and the chemical systems that control our mood and behaviour. For example, vascular diseases (those affecting the blood vessels) and Parkinson's disease damage important areas of the brain, making people vulnerable to depression and perhaps triggering the illness.

Endocrine conditions directly interact with, and upset, important chemical systems governing mood and other features of depressive illness.

However, the psychological and social impacts of the illness are also very important. Suddenly losing function in a limb after a stroke, or struggling to walk after a heart attack, can lead to a number of social consequences – being unable to return to work, having to give up certain hobbies, etc. Such losses may trigger a depressive illness.

At the same time, these losses affect the sufferer's self-esteem and their roles at home and work may be changed, too. These factors may all contribute to the development of depression.

What should you do if someone is depressed and physically ill?

- Try to encourage the person to talk about their feelings and

difficulties, because support from friends and family is important and not to be underestimated.
- However, if depression is suspected then you should seek help, usually through the family doctor (GP).
- The treatment of depression in somebody who is physically ill may include talking therapies and/or antidepressants.
- Support groups for the specific physical illnesses can be sources of information and understanding.

- The above information is reprinted with kind permission from Net Doctor. Visit www.netdoctor.co.uk for more information.

© Net Doctor

Are you at risk for depression?

Information from Wing of Madness

Most people know the risk factors for illnesses such as heart disease or high blood pressure, but not many people realize that clinical depression has risk factors associated with it also. Having these risk factors doesn't mean you will suffer from depression, only that you may be predisposed to it. Below, in no particular order, are listed some of these risk factors.

- There is a history of mental illness in your family.
- You are a woman. One in four women suffers from depression at some point in her life.
- You were sexually abused as a child.
- Someone close to you is depressed (depression can be 'contagious').
- You have a chronic illness or are in chronic pain.
- You lost a parent at an early age, either through death or abandonment.
- You have heart disease. One in five heart patients has severe depression.
- Someone close to you has recently died, or you are experiencing another stressful life event such as divorce or financial problems.
- You are taking a medication that has depression as a side-effect.

- The above information is reprinted with kind permission from Wing of Madness. Visit www.wingofmadness.com for more information.

© Wing of Madness

Depression is UK's biggest social problem

Expert advocates a network of 250 centres across the country to offer psychological therapies

Depression, anxiety and other forms of mental illness have taken over from unemployment as the greatest social problem in the UK, a health economist warns today.

Richard Layard, who is advising the government on mental health, advocates a network of 250 centres across the country to offer psychological therapies – instead of the drugs widely handed out by doctors in the absence of sufficient therapists.

Only 4% of all those with depression and anxiety disorders received psychological therapy in the past year

Around 15% of the population suffers from depression or anxiety, says Lord Layard, Emeritus Professor at the Centre for Economic Performance of the London School of Economics. The economic cost in terms of lost productivity is huge – around £17bn, or 1.5% of UK gross domestic product. 'There are now more than 1 million mentally ill people receiving incapacity benefits – more than the total number of unemployed people receiving unemployment benefits,' he writes in the *British Medical Journal*.

'Yet if you have one of these often crippling conditions you are unlikely to get any specialist help at all. You can see your GP, but he or she is unlikely to prescribe any treatment other than drugs.'

The National Institute for Clinical Excellence (NICE) has advised that drugs are not the best answer.

By Sarah Boseley, Health Editor

They may work in adults in the short term, but patients more easily relapse when they stop taking them, and may suffer side-effects. The Medicines and Healthcare Products Regulatory Authority (MHRA), which licenses drugs, has told doctors not to prescribe most of the modern antidepressants known as the SSRIs (selective serotonin re-uptake inhibitors), like Seroxat, to under-18s because risks outweigh benefits.

Only 4% of all those with depression and anxiety disorders received psychological therapy in the past year, Lord Layard says. Yet the 'talking' therapies are popular with patients who often do not want drugs.

Lord Layard says the cost of therapy is about £750 for each patient. In the next two years it is likely he or she will have about 12 extra months free of illness compared with no treatment, and at least one extra month in work worth more than £1,880, he says, which more than pays the £750 cost of treatment. There are other financial benefits too, he says, which include fewer needing to be hospitalised.

Lord Layard says: 'It is important for the government to begin by envisaging what kind of provision is necessary and only after that to consider how fast it could be established.' He estimates that around 800,000 patients a year would require cognitive behaviour therapy. That means the country needs an extra 10,000 therapists.

A department spokeswoman said two 'demonstration sites' aimed at increasing access to psychological therapies would be launched soon.
28 April 2006

Teenage depression

Sometimes it's difficult to tell if your child is suffering from teenage angst or is really depressed. Liz Bestic gives guidance on spotting the signs of depression

Anyone living with a teenager knows that life is often a rollercoaster of emotional highs and lows. Luckily, most teenagers manage to navigate their way through the stormy waters of adolescence without coming to any harm. But, according to the mental health charity, Depression Alliance, statistics on teenage depression are pretty scary. There are currently more than two million children attending GP's surgeries with various forms of psychological or emotional problems, and more than 19,000 adolescents attempt suicide every year – that's more than one every half an hour.

> ## More than 19,000 adolescents attempt suicide every year – that's more than one every half an hour

Coping with life's ups and downs

A recent study by the Mental Health Foundation also found that children today are less resilient and less able to cope with the ups and downs of life, which is no help if you are wondering whether your teenager is really depressed or just suffering from typical teenage angst. 'If a young person comes to my surgery saying they can't get out of bed in the morning, feel exhausted and can't concentrate at school I would say they were depressed and need help,' says GP Chris Manning, Co-chair of Depression Alliance.

Joanne Morgan knows exactly what he means. Last year her 15-year-old daughter Mandy dropped out of school. She retreated to her bedroom and lost all interest in life. 'She couldn't cope with exams and

By Liz Bestic

schoolwork, had no motivation at all and felt tired all the time,' says Joanne. 'I took her to the GP, who diagnosed depression and put her on a course of antidepressants, which lifted her mood for a while. But it was really only when she had some professional counselling that she began to work out why she felt so low,' explains Joanne.

Antidepressants for adolescents

Depression in children and teenagers is on a spectrum: mild, moderate and severe. At the lower end of the spectrum, therapy may be all that is required to help a child over a difficult period. Drugs are only normally necessary when depression is so severe that the young person is at risk. Although the new wave of antidepressants known as SSRIs (selective serotonin re-uptake inhibitors) are widely used for adults, many doctors are reluctant to prescribe them for adolescents.

Professor Peter Hill, consultant psychiatrist at Great Ormond Street Hospital, thinks doctors are not sufficiently aware that antidepressants can be extremely helpful. He would not hesitate to prescribe them in serious cases. 'If you are faced with someone who may kill themselves in the next 48 hours you have to make tough decisions. There is good evidence that SSRIs are very effective in teenage depression,' he adds.

Keep talking

According to experts, the most important thing to do is keep all lines of communication with your child open. Encourage them to share their thoughts and feelings with you, and recognise their concerns without judging them. 'Face the problem together and do whatever it

takes to get them through,' explains Peter Wilson from the children's mental health charity, Young Minds. 'Tell them your own experiences of adolescence, so they can see that things can end positively. And, above all never, never underestimate any threats or attempts to hurt themselves,' he adds.

How to tell if your child is depressed

According to Young Minds, if your child has experienced three or more of the symptoms below, and has felt this way for more than two weeks, seek help immediately:

- sleeps too much or too little;
- nothing feels good any more;
- no interest in food or eating too much;
- feeling down;
- lack of self confidence;
- agitation;
- great anxiety;
- difficulty concentrating;
- feeling guilty about things;
- feeling tired all the time;
- feeling that life is pointless;
- feeling tearful.

- The above information is reprinted with kind permission from iVillage UK. Visit www.iVillage.co.uk for more information.

© iVillage UK

Depression and underage drinking

One child in 10 has depression and drinking is partly to blame

More than a million children are suffering in an epidemic of depression and anxiety, a disturbing report revealed yesterday.

One in 10 youngsters under 16 has a mental health disorder, according to the British Medical Association (BMA). Many need help with depression, anxiety or eating disorders. Other problems include hyperactivity disorders, excessive temper tantrums and, in extreme cases, self-harm and suicide attempts.

A sharp increase in binge drinking, particularly among young girls, has contributed to the rise in disorders said the BMA.

A 2004 survey of 11 to 15-year-olds found that around a quarter said they drank an average of 10.7 units a week – equivalent to five pints of beer. In 1990, the higher-drinking group averaged only 5.3 units.

> **A 2004 survey of 11 to 15-year-olds found that around a quarter said they drank an average of 10.7 units a week – equivalent to five pints of beer**

The growing number of children from broken homes are also at a higher risk of developing mental health problems, as are children from poor backgrounds and asylum seekers. The report accused mental health services of failing vulnerable children, in particular those in care and those from black and ethnic minority backgrounds.

This is due to a 'worrying shortage' of mental health professionals and

By Emily Cook,
Health Reporter

a lack of adequate funding and services.

The BMA called for improved services for children in care and said racism within mental health services must be eliminated.

> **One in 10 youngsters under 16 has a mental health disorder, according to the British Medical Association**

Dr Vivienne Nathanson, the Association's head of ethics and science, said: 'Children from deprived backgrounds have a poorer start on many levels. Without good mental health they may not have a chance to develop emotionally and reach their full potential.

There are a number of government policies being rolled out that are aimed at tackling these problems. It is essential they deliver what they promise.'

Emotional disorders are the most common mental health problems. It is estimated that 1 per cent of children and 3 per cent of adolescents suffer from depression in any one year. Self-harm is also on the increase – with 11.2 per cent of girls and 3.2 per cent of boys committing acts such as cutting, burning or self-poisoning themselves as a means of coping.

Girls tend to suffer from emotional disorders such as anorexia and bulimia, while boys are more likely to have a 'conduct disorder' – which may include severe tantrums, persistent disobedience and fighting.

Marjorie Wallace, Chief Executive of the mental health charity Sane, said: 'It is vital that all children and young people with mental health problems are identified and treated from the earliest stage.

'It is this group that is most at risk of lifelong and life-threatening psychiatric disorder yet, as this report again highlights, families struggle to get the help they need.'

Dr Marcus Roberts, Head of Policy at the charity Mind, said: 'It's crucial that the right kind of services are there to break what can become a cycle, where poverty contributes to mental distress, which in turn leads to unemployment, stigma and further poverty.'

The Department of Health said the number of staff in child and adolescent mental health services and the number of cases handled had both increased by more than 40 per cent between 2002 and 2005.

A spokesman added: 'In the last three years £300million has been invested in child and adolescent mental health services.'

■ This article was first published in the Daily Mail, 21 June 2006.

Ecstasy and depression

Does ecstasy use cause long-term mental health problems? The current research is inconclusive, but that doesn't mean everything is rosy

What do we know about ecstasy?

Ecstasy (MDMA) works by stimulating the production of a chemical called serotonin in the brain. The rush you get comes from the release of much higher levels of serotonin than normal. But by artificially messing with this production process, some scientists believe users are diminishing their brain's ability to produce serotonin in the future.

Short-term effects

It's estimated almost half a million people regularly use ecstasy in Britain, generally without reporting much short-term mental health damage. While up, some people suffer from paranoia, confusion or anxiety while in the days that follow, the worst that most people suffer is minor depression. It's important to note that this isn't the case for everyone; other factors play a part in how a person reacts to ecstasy use including diet, general state of health and their genetic make-up. It also depends on how often and how much ecstasy you take.

Long-term effects

In drug terms, ecstasy is still a relatively young drug. Consequently, it's only recently that scientists could begin to evaluate the drug's long-term effects.

Although some argue that of the 'original' ecstasy users, few have shown signs of long-term damage, many scientists are less convinced. Recent studies have reported a number of frightening problems associated with long-term use, including memory problems, severe sleep problems and major depression.

A *Mixmag* magazine survey found that regular ecstasy users are 25% more likely to suffer a mental health disorder than the rest of the population and were twice as likely to have seen a doctor about mental health issues, with half of those being concerned about depression.

Further research is needed before any major conclusions can be reached, but regular ecstasy users should understand that the evidence doesn't look good.

■ The above information is reprinted with kind permission from TheSite.org. For more information, please visit their website at www. thesite.org

© *TheSite.org*

Depression and suicide

An overview

■ Depression is a very common mental health problem worldwide. It is estimated that it will become the second most common cause of disability, after heart disease, by 2020.

■ The term 'depression' covers a very wide range of experiences and level of illness forms, from mild to severe, transient to persistent.

■ A distinction should be made between 'unipolar' forms of depression such as major depression and dysthymia which involve persistent, low moods, and manic or 'bipolar' depression which involves bouts of low moods followed by extreme 'highs' or mania.

■ Unipolar forms of depression are more common in women than men. In Britain, 3 to 4% of men and 7 to 8% of women suffer from moderate to severe depression at any one time.

■ Bipolar depression affects men and women equally, and afflicts about five people in 1,000.

■ For people with severe depression, the lifetime risk of suicide may be as high as 6%. This compares with a risk of 1.3% in the general population.

■ For those with bipolar, suicide risks are high, at 15 times that of the general population.

■ Antidepressants can be very effective in helping people to recover from depression, but can also be used to attempt suicide through an overdose. There is no evidence to show that they reduce suicide or self-harm.

■ Selective serotonin re-uptake inhibitors have been investigated as antidepressant drugs which can cause suicidal thoughts and behaviour in some people. Current research suggests that this is true for children and adolescents but there is no evidence to support the heightened suicide risk in adults.

■ Symptoms of depression appear over a period or in the case of manic depression, suddenly and escalate over a few days.

■ The above information is reprinted with kind permission from the Samaritans. Visit www.samaritans.org.uk for more information.

© *Samaritans*

New reports link mental ill-health to changing diets

Information from the Mental Health Foundation

As new figures show that mental ill-health is costing the UK almost £100 billion a year, evidence released today by the Mental Health Foundation and Sustain reveals that changes to the human diet in the last 50 years or so could be an important factor behind the major rise of mental ill-health in the UK.

A body of evidence linking the impact of diet on mood and behaviour has been growing for many years. Now scientific evidence, published today, reveals that food can have an immediate and lasting effect upon a person's mental health and behaviour because of the way it affects the structure and function of the brain.

A deficiency in certain amino acids can lead to feelings of depression, apathy and leave a person feeling unmotivated and unable to relax

Significant changes in the way food is produced and manufactured have not only reduced the amounts of essential fats, vitamins and minerals consumed, but have also disturbed the balance of nutrients in the foods eaten. The proliferation of industrialised farming has introduced pesticides and altered the body fat composition of animals due to the diets they are now fed. As a result, the population's intake of omega-3 fatty acids has decreased whilst the consumption of omega-6 fatty acids has increased. According to the research, this unequal intake combined with a lack of vitamins and minerals is associated with depression, concentration and memory problems.

New figures show that mental ill-health is costing the UK almost £100 billion a year

At the same time, the UK population is consuming less nutritious, fresh produce and more saturated fats and sugars. According to the Mental Health Foundation and Sustain, new substances, such as pesticides, additives and trans-fats have also been introduced to the diet. These, alone and in combination, can prevent the brain from functioning effectively.

There have also been remarkable changes in the way that the population prepares and cooks food. The research shows that only 29 per cent of 15 to 24 year olds report eating a meal made from scratch every day, compared to 50 per cent of those aged over 65. It is also reported that a high proportion of younger people are eating insufficient amounts of fresh fruit and vegetables, instead eating unhealthy foods including ready meals and takeaways.

Amino acids are vital to good mental health. Neurotransmitters in the brain are made from amino acids, many of which need to be derived from the diet. A deficiency in certain amino acids can lead to feelings of depression, apathy and leave a person feeling unmotivated and unable to relax.

The two charities assert that many nutrients can improve a person's mental health, and dietary changes may hold the key to combating specific mental health problems including depression, schizophrenia, attention-deficit hyperactivity disorder (ADHD), and Alzheimer's disease.

Dr Andrew McCulloch, Chief Executive of the Mental Health Foundation, says:

'We are well aware of the effect of diet upon our physical health, but we are only just beginning to understand how the brain, as an organ, is influenced by the nutrients it derives from the foods we eat, and how our diets have an impact on our mental health. This evidence raises a number of important questions and concerns for us all, but the knowledge gives individuals the power to make decisions that will benefit them and future generations. On a larger scale, our government cannot ignore the growing burden of mental ill-health in the UK and must look to nutrition as an option in helping people to manage their mental health problems. The potential rewards, in economic terms, and in terms of alleviating human suffering, are enormous.'

Courtney Van de Weyer, researcher on the Feeding Minds campaign at Sustain, added:

'The good news is that the diet for a healthy mind is the same as the diet for a health body. The bad news is that, unless there is a radical overhaul of food and farming policies – particularly on fish – there won't be healthy and nutritious foods available in the future for people to eat.'

The two charities have joined forces on the 'Feeding Minds' campaign to raise awareness of the links between diet and mental health, and are asking the government to increase financial and political support for measures to ensure that sustainable supplies of a wide variety of nutrient-rich foods are available, affordable and attractive for people to obtain both now and in the future. They are also calling on the Government to incorporate the link between diet and mental health into all food-related policy and practice.

Report key findings

Food consumption

- Over the last 60 years there has been a 34 per cent decline in UK vegetable consumption, with currently only 13 per cent of men and 15 per cent of women now eating at least five portions of fruit and vegetables per day.
- People in the UK eat 59 per cent less fish – the main source of omega 3 fatty acids – than they did 60 years ago.

Mental health

- Some foods damage the brain by releasing toxins or oxidants that harm healthy brain cells. There are many more nutrients that serve the brain without deception or damage, which can improve mood and mental well-being.
- A balanced mood and feelings of well-being can be protected by ensuring that a diet provides adequate amounts of complex carbohydrates, essential fats, amino acids, vitamins and minerals and water.
- Research indicates that good nutritional intake may be linked to academic success. A number of studies report that providing children with breakfast improves their daily and long-term academic performance.
- Among some young offenders, diets supplemented with vitamins, minerals and essential fatty acids have resulted in significant and remarkable reductions in anti-social behaviour.

Mental health problems

- There is growing evidence that diet plays an important contributory role in specific mental health problems including ADHD, depression, schizophrenia and Alzheimer's disease.
- The presentation of depression in the UK population has increased dramatically over recent decades and this has been accompanied by a decrease in the age of onset, with more cases being reported in children, adolescents and young adults.
- The incidence of schizophrenia is similar across the globe, although there are differences in outcomes between countries. This implies that environmental factors have some role in determining the duration and severity of symptoms, and the role that diet has to play is attracting increasing scientific interest.
- Alzheimer's disease has become more common in the past 50 years and is believed to be the result of a combination of factors, including the aging population, genetics and environmental factors. Growing epidemiological evidence suggests that diet may be one of those environmental factors, with associations being reported between the occurrence of Alzheimer's and high saturated fat, consumption, and low vitamin and mineral consumption.
- Complementary mental health care services that focus on diet and nutrition report promising results, particularly among those who experience ADHD and depression. On the whole however, they are poorly funded and have received insufficient research attention to draw firm conclusions.

National opinion poll findings

- Women report eating healthy foods, including fresh vegetables, fruit or fruit juice and meals made from scratch more often than men, who tend to eat more takeaways and ready meals.
- Younger people are more likely than older people to report daily mental health problems, as are those in social class DE, those on a lower income, those who are not in paid employment and those who are not married.
- Nearly two-thirds of those who do not report daily mental health problems eat fresh fruit or fruit juice every day, compared with less than half of those who do report daily mental health problems. This pattern is similar for fresh vegetables and salad.
- Those who report some level of mental health problem also eat fewer healthy foods (fresh fruit and vegetables, organic foods and meals made from scratch) and more unhealthy foods (chips and crisps, chocolate, ready meals and takeaways).

16 January 2006

- The above information is reprinted with kind permission from the Mental Health Foundation. Visit www.mentalhealth.org.uk for more information.

© *Mental Health Foundation*

Men and depression

Information from the Royal College of Psychiatrists

Introduction

This article is for any man who is depressed, their friends and their family. Men seem to suffer from depression just as often as women, but they are less likely to ask for help. This leaflet gives some basic facts about depression, how it affects men in particular, and how to get help.

Why is it important?

Depression causes a huge amount of suffering. It is a major reason for people taking time off work. Many people who kill themselves have been depressed – so it is potentially fatal. However, it is easy to treat, and this is best done as early as possible.

There is evidence that some symptoms of depression are more common in men than in women. Men are also more likely to commit suicide

---

What's the difference between just feeling miserable and being depressed?

Everyone has times in their lives when they feel down or depressed. It is usually for a good reason, does not dominate your life and does not last for a long time. However, if the depression goes on for a long time, or becomes very severe, you may find yourself stuck and unable to lift yourself out of the depression. This is what doctors call a 'depressive illness'. Some people suffer from manic depression (also called bipolar affective disorder). They have periods of bad depression, but also times of great 'elation' and over-activity. These can be just as harmful as the periods of depression. (See the Royal College of Psychiatrists' leaflet on Manic Depression/Bipolar disorder.)

What are the signs and symptoms?

If you are depressed, you will probably notice some of the following:

Mind

You:

- feel unhappy, miserable, down, depressed. It just won't go away and can be worse at a particular time of day, often first thing in the morning;
- can't enjoy anything;
- can't concentrate properly;
- feel guilty about things that have nothing to do with you;
- become pessimistic;
- start to feel hopeless, and perhaps even suicidal.

Body

You:

- can't get to sleep, and wake early in the morning and/or throughout the night;
- lose interest in sex;
- can't eat;
- lose weight.

Other people may notice that you:

- perform less well at work;
- seem unusually quiet and unable to talk about things;
- worry about things more than usual;
- are more irritable than usual;
- complain more about vague physical problems;
- are not looking after yourself properly – you may not bother to shave, wash your hair, look after your clothes.

How is depression different for men?

There is no evidence for a completely separate type of 'male depression'. However, there is evidence that some symptoms of depression are more common in men than in women. These include:

- irritability;
- sudden anger;
- increased loss of control;
- greater risk-taking;
- aggression.

Men are also more likely to commit suicide.

Getting help

Men seem to suffer from depression just as often as women, but are less likely to ask for help. It may also be that men try to deal with their depression by using drugs and alcohol. This might account for the fact that, although men are diagnosed as having depression less than women, they abuse drugs and alcohol rather more.

Men's attitudes and behaviour

Compared with women, men tend to be more competitive and concerned with power and success. Most men don't like to admit that they feel fragile or that they need help. They feel that they should rely on themselves, and that it is somehow weak to have to depend on someone else, even for a short time. So they are less likely to talk about their feelings with their friends, loved ones or their doctors. This may be why they don't get the help they need.

This traditional view of how men should be – always tough and self-reliant – is also held by some women. Some men worry that, if they talk about their feelings of depression, their partner may reject them. Even professionals may share this view, and do not spot depression in men as often as they should.

How do men cope?

Instead of talking about how they feel, men may use alcohol or drugs to feel better. This usually makes things worse, certainly in the long run. Your work will suffer and alcohol often leads to irresponsible, unpleasant or dangerous behaviour. Men may also focus more on their work than their relationships or home life. This can cause conflicts with your wife or partner. All of these things make depression more likely.

Relationships

For married men, research has shown that trouble in a marriage or long-term relationship is the single most common problem associated with depression. Men can't cope with disagreements as well as women. Arguments actually make men feel very physically uncomfortable. They try to avoid arguments or difficult discussions. The partner will want to talk about a problem, but he will do his best to avoid it. The partner then feels ignored and tries to talk about it more, which makes the man feel he is being nagged. So, he withdraws further, which makes his partner feel even more ignored and

so on. This vicious circle can destroy a relationship.

Separation and divorce

Men have traditionally seen themselves as being in control of their families' lives. However, the process of separation and divorce is most often started by women. Of all men, those who are divorced are most likely to kill themselves, probably because depression is more common and more severe in this group. This may be because, as well as losing their main relationship:

- they often lose touch with their children
- they may have to move to live in a different place
- they often find themselves short of money.

Instead of talking about how they feel, men may use alcohol or drugs to feel better. This usually makes things worse, certainly in the long run

---

These are stressful events in themselves, quite apart from the stress of the break-up, and may bring on depression.

Sex

When men are depressed, they feel less good about their bodies and less sexy. Many go off sex completely. Several recent studies suggest that, in spite of this, men who are depressed have intercourse just as often, but they don't feel as satisfied as usual. A few depressed men actually report an increase in sexual drive and intercourse, possibly as a way of trying to make themselves feel better. Another problem may be that some antidepressant drugs reduce sex-drive in a small number of men. However, the good news is that, as the depression improves, so will sexual desire, performance and satisfaction.

It's worth remembering that it can happen the other way round. Impotence (difficulty in getting or

keeping an erection) can bring about depression. Again, this is a problem for which it is usually possible to find effective help.

Pregnancy and children

We have known for many years that some mothers feel severely depressed after having a baby. It is only recently that we have realised that more than one in 10 fathers also suffer psychological problems during this time. This shouldn't really be surprising. We know that major events in people's lives, even good ones like moving house, can make you depressed. And this particular event changes your life more than any other. Suddenly, you have to spend much more of your time looking after your partner, and possibly other children, and you may be very tired.

On an intimate level, new mothers tend to be less interested in sex for a number of months. Simple tiredness is the main problem, although you may take it personally and feel that you are being rejected. You may have to adjust, perhaps for the first time, to taking second place in your partner's affections. You may also find that you can't spend so much time at work.

New fathers are more likely to become depressed if their partner is depressed, if they aren't getting on with their partner, or if they are unemployed. This isn't important just from the father's point of view. It will affect the mother and may have an impact on how the baby grows and develops in the first few months.

Unemployment and retirement

Leaving work, for any reason, can be stressful. Recent research has shown that up to one in seven men who become unemployed will develop a depressive illness in the next six months.

After relationship difficulties, unemployment is the thing most likely to push a man into a serious depression – work is often the main source of a man's sense of worth and self-esteem. You may lose the signs of your success, such as the company car. You may have to adjust to being at home, looking after children, while your wife or partner becomes the breadwinner.

From a position of being in control, you may face a future over which you have little, especially if it takes a long time to find another job.

You are more likely to become depressed if you are shy, if you don't have a close relationship or if you don't manage to find another job. Depression itself can make it harder to get another job.

Men are around three times more likely to kill themselves than women. Suicide is commonest among men who are separated, widowed or divorced and is more likely if someone is a heavy drinker

---

Even retiring from work at the usual age can be difficult for many men, especially if your partner continues to work. It can be hard to adjust to losing the structure of your day and your contact with colleagues.

Gay men and depression

On the whole, gay men do not suffer from depression any more than straight men. However, it seems that gay teenagers and young adults are more likely to become depressed, possibly due to the stress of 'coming out'.

Suicide

Men are around three times more likely to kill themselves than women. Suicide is commonest among men who are separated, widowed or divorced and is more likely if someone is a heavy drinker.

Over the last few years, men have become more likely to kill themselves, particularly those aged between 16 and 24 years and those between 39 and 54 years. We don't yet know the reason for this.

We do know that around half the people who kill themselves will have seen their GP in the previous four weeks – although not necessarily to discuss their emotional state. However, fewer men than women will have seen their GP in the year before their suicide. We also know that about two out of three people who kill themselves will have talked about it to friends or family.

Asking someone if he is feeling suicidal will not put the idea into his head or make it more likely that he will kill himself. Even if someone is not very good at talking about how he is feeling, it is important to ask if you have any suspicion – and to take such ideas seriously.

For a man who feels suicidal, there is nothing more demoralising than to feel that others do not take him seriously. He will often have taken some time to pluck up the courage to tell anyone about it.

If you find yourself feeling so bad that you have thought about suicide, it can be a great relief to talk about it.

Violence

Some studies have shown that men who commit violent crimes are more likely to get depressed than men who don't. However, we don't know if the depression makes their violence more likely, or if it's just the way they lead their lives.

Helping men

Many men find it difficult to ask for help when they are depressed – it can feel unmanly and weak. It may be easier for men to ask for help if those who give that help take into account men's special needs.

Men who are depressed are more likely to talk about the physical symptoms of their depression than the emotional and psychological ones. This may be one reason why doctors sometimes don't diagnose it. If you are feeling wretched, don't hold back – tell your GP.

It can help to see depression as a result of chemical changes in the brain and/or as the inevitable cost of living in a demanding and difficult world. It is nothing to do with being weak or unmanly and it can be helped. Both talking and medication can be important ways to help you get better.

If a depressed man is married, or in a steady relationship – straight or gay – his partner should be involved so that she/he can understand what is happening. This will make it less likely for the depression to interfere with their relationship.

Some men don't feel comfortable talking about themselves, and so may be reluctant to consider psychotherapy. However, it is a powerful way of relieving depression and works well for many men.

■ The above information is an extract from the Royal College of Psychiatrists' factsheet 'Men and Depression' and is reprinted with permission. For more information, please visit their website at www.rcpsych.ac.uk.

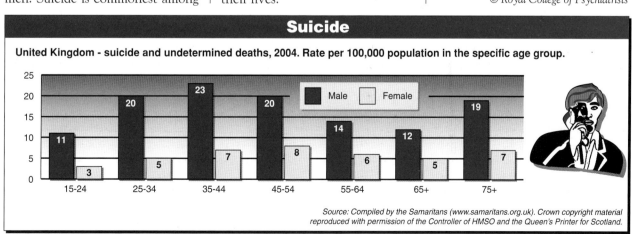

Suicide

United Kingdom - suicide and undetermined deaths, 2004. Rate per 100,000 population in the specific age group.

Age group	Male	Female
15-24	11	3
25-34	20	5
35-44	23	7
45-54	20	8
55-64	14	6
65+	12	5
75+	19	7

Source: Compiled by the Samaritans (www.samaritans.org.uk). Crown copyright material reproduced with permission of the Controller of HMSO and the Queen's Printer for Scotland.

Statistics on mental health

Some quick facts

How many people in the UK have a mental health problem?

- One in four people will experience some kind of mental health problem in the course of a year.

What are the main types of mental health problems?

- One in six people will have depression at some point in their life. Depression is most common in people aged 25 to 44 years.
- One in 10 people are likely to have a 'disabling anxiety disorder' at some stage in their life. For manic depression and schizophrenia this figure is one in 100.

Who develops mental health problems?

- 20 per cent of women and 14 per cent of men in England have some form of mental illness.

One in six people will have depression at some point in their life. Depression is most common in people aged 25 to 44 years

- 18 per cent of women have a 'neurotic disorder' such as anxiety, depression, phobias and panic attacks, compared with 11 per cent of men.
- Men are three times more likely than women to have alcohol dependence and twice as likely to be dependent on drugs.

What about mental health problems among children and young people?

- 15 per cent of pre-school children will have mild mental health problems and 7 per cent will have severe mental health problems.

- 6 per cent of boys and 16 per cent of girls aged 16 to 19 are thought to have some form of mental health problem.

What is the prevalence of mental health problems in older people?

- 15 per cent of people over 65 have depression.
- Up to 670,000 people in the UK have some form of dementia. Five per cent of people over 65 and 10 to 20 per cent of people over 80 have dementia.

What about suicide and self-harm?

- 75 per cent of all suicides are by men.
- 20 per cent of all deaths by young people are by suicide.
- 17 per cent of all suicides are by people aged 65 or over.
- Approximately 142,000 hospital admissions each year in England and Wales are the result of deliberate self-harm. Approximately 19,000 of these are young people.

- Self-harm is more common in women than in men.

What is the relationship between mental health problems and offending?

- 10 to 20 per cent of young people involved in criminal activity are thought to have a 'psychiatric disorder'.
- In England and Wales an estimated 66 per cent of the remand population had mental health problems, compared with 39 per cent of the sentenced population.

What are the costs of mental health problems?

- The total cost of mental health problems in England has been estimated at £32 billion. More than one-third of this cost (almost £12 billion) is attributed to lost employment and productivity related to schizophrenia, depression, stress and anxiety.
- Over 91 million working days are lost to mental ill-health every year. Half of the days lost through mental illness are due to anxiety and stress conditions.

Updated 2 July 2003

- The above information is reprinted with kind permission from the Mental Health Foundation. Visit www.mentalhealth.org.uk for more information.

ONE IN FOUR...

Post-natal depression

Information from Parentline Plus

Post-natal depression is very common, affecting at least one in ten new mothers, but many can suffer in silence because their condition is not recognised or dismissed as simply the 'baby blues'.

Post-natal depression is an illness, and although it is not known for certain what causes it, some experts believe that the sudden change in hormones after the birth may trigger the condition. Getting post-natal depression is not failing, nor is it related to how capable a person is, it is an illness.

Post-natal depression is often viewed with shame by sufferers who may feel a 'failure' or a 'bad mother' because they feel unable to cope

---

It usually develops within the first four to six weeks, but can start even several months following childbirth and can emerge at any time during the first year. It comes on either gradually or all of a sudden, and can range from being relatively mild to hard-hitting.

Post-natal depression is still an illness that is not widely understood by mums who experience it or by their family and friends. In fact, it is often viewed with shame by sufferers who may feel a 'failure' or a 'bad mother' because they feel unable to cope. In fact, the opposite is true, with all the evidence showing that mothers with post-natal illness are at least as good at mothering as those without.

Symptoms of post-natal depression

- Crying a lot, often over the smallest things.
- Poor concentration.
- Anxiety.

Parentline plus

- Guilt.
- Lack of confidence in her ability as a mother.
- Not enjoying motherhood.
- Loss of appetite or overeating.
- Extreme tiredness.
- Irritability.
- Fear of harming herself or the baby, though the reality is that only in very rare cases is anyone harmed.
- Sleeping problems.
- No interest in sex.
- Being hostile or indifferent to your husband or partner.
- A sense of being overwhelmed and unable to cope.
- Difficulty in making decisions or concentrating.
- Physical symptoms, such as stomach pains, headaches and blurred vision.

Diagnosis

The diagnosis is usually made by a doctor based on what those who know you, tell him or her. Sometimes the doctor may do a blood test to rule out physical reasons for the symptoms, such as anaemia. A short questionnaire has been developed called the Edinburgh Post-Natal Depression Scale and has 10 simple questions. Doctors and health visitors may ask a patient to fill it in if they suspect post-natal depression.

Treatments for post-natal depression

Self-help
The most important thing you can do for yourself is believe that you will get better.

- Try to get as much rest as you can although this can be difficult with a small baby. Try to recruit the help of friends or family and readily accept any offers of help that come along. This is very important, as tiredness seems to make depression worse.
- Don't try to force yourself back to normal too quickly. Many mothers feel that by keeping busy such as going back to work, things will right themselves, but this can actually prolong the illness.
- Be kind to yourself. Don't force yourself to do things you don't

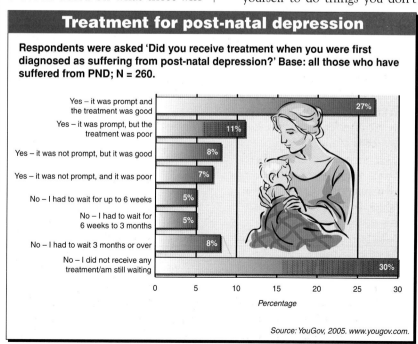

Treatment for post-natal depression

Respondents were asked 'Did you receive treatment when you were first diagnosed as suffering from post-natal depression?' Base: all those who have suffered from PND; N = 260.

Response	Percentage
Yes – it was prompt and the treatment was good	27%
Yes – it was prompt, but the treatment was poor	11%
Yes – it was not prompt, but it was good	8%
Yes – it was not prompt, and it was poor	7%
No – I had to wait for up to 6 weeks	5%
No – I had to wait for 6 weeks to 3 months	5%
No – I had to wait 3 months or over	8%
No – I did not receive any treatment/am still waiting	30%

Percentage

Source: YouGov, 2005. www.yougov.com.

really want to do or that upset you.

- Exercise. It can be difficult to be active when all you want to do is curl up and go to sleep but exercise releases endorphins.

Possible sources of help include the GP, midwife, health visitor, community psychiatric nurse, psychotherapist, counsellor or psychiatrist.

Experts suggest that the best treatment for post-natal depression may be a combination of practical support and advice, psychotherapy, counselling and, if necessary, antidepressants.

Support and advice

Support and understanding from friends and relatives can help recovery and it is far better to talk about your feelings rather than bottling them up. Ask your health visitor about what is available in the area, such as self-help or support groups which can provide lots of encouragement and advice.

Counselling

These treatments can be very effective and offer you the opportunity to explore any underlying factors that could have contributed to the post-natal depression. Although the availability of counselling can depend on where you live, many GPs now have a counsellor or psychotherapist attached to their surgery. They can also refer to a psychologist or psychiatrist on the NHS.

Antidepressants

Many mothers, particularly those with milder symptoms, recover without antidepressants, but they can be very effective for post-natal depression.

A GP can prescribe different kinds of medication to help and it is important to discuss all the options fully beforehand. They can take a month or two to start working effectively, although if you don't feel any benefits during that time, see your doctor again and he or she may need to try a different drug or adjust the medication.

It's also important to remember that any medication can enter the breast milk and this will be a major consideration.

- Information from Parentline Plus. Visit www.parentlineplus.org.uk for more information.

© *Parentline Plus*

Feeling SAD?

SAD stands for seasonal affective disorder. Although most people feel a little down when winter hits, SAD sufferers have symptoms that are severe enough to disrupt their lives

Symptoms

- Problems sleeping: oversleeping but not feeling refreshed, unable to get out of bed, needing a nap in the afternoon.
- Overeating: carbohydrate craving leading to weight gain.
- Depression: despair, misery, guilt, anxiety, normal tasks become frustratingly difficult, hopelessness.
- Family problems: avoiding your family and friends, irritability, loss of libido, feeling emotionally numb.
- Lethargy: too tired to cope, everything becomes an effort.
- Physical symptoms: often joint pain or stomach problems and a lowered resistance to infection.
- Behavioural problems: especially in younger people.

When does it start?

The symptoms tend to start in September and last until April.

TheSite.org

They are at their worst in the darkest months.

What causes it?

Apparently it stems from the lack of bright light in winter.

Who does it affect?

Roughly 2% of the population of Northern Europe suffer badly, with many more suffering milder cases. Across the world the incidence increases with distance from the equator, except where there is snow on the ground, when it becomes less common. More women than men are diagnosed as having SAD. Children and adolescents are also vulnerable.

What treatment is there?

A perfect cure is going to a brightly-lit climate, whether skiing or somewhere hot (any excuse for a holiday!).

Otherwise, exposure to bright light every day by using a light box or a similar bright light therapy device may help. For most people sitting in front of a light box for between 15 and 45 minutes a day, allowing the light to reach their eyes, will be sufficient to alleviate the symptoms. Some sufferers also need treatment with antidepressant medication.

Should I talk to my doctor?

Yes. They can tell you where the NHS specialist SAD clinics are in the UK, and help you seek treatment.

- The above information is reprinted with kind permission from TheSite.org. Visit www.thesite.org for more information.

© *TheSite.org*

Manic depression

Information from SANE

This factsheet aims to explain manic depression (also called bipolar disorder). You will find a description of the condition, its symptoms and the treatments available. If you are experiencing manic depression, you will find suggestions of ways that you may help yourself and the options open to you. You will also find ideas on how friends and family may help.

What is manic depression?

Manic depression is a major mental health problem. People diagnosed with manic depression tend to experience mood swings from periods of severe depression to periods of elation known as mania. Most people experience ups and downs in daily life, but with manic depression the changes between highs and lows are extreme. It is known as a psychotic illness because people can lose touch with reality.

What are the symptoms of manic depression?

Mania

If you are experiencing a manic phase you may feel marvellous, on a high, excitable and euphoric. In manic states, people can lose insight and may experience delusions. For example, people may think that they are famous and important. They may make wild plans, spend extravagantly and lose social inhibitions. In manic phases, people may lose insight into the fact that they are ill and deny that there is anything wrong with them or their behaviour.

Depression

If you are experiencing a depressive phase, you may feel unhappy, that everything you do is a struggle, and perhaps not worth the effort. Often people feel hopeless about the future and unable to see any positives in life. You may feel apathetic and unable to participate in activities you used to enjoy. At its worst, depression can lead to such feelings of helplessness and lack of worth that people may give up the will to live, or begin to consider suicide.

What causes manic depression?

There is no single cause of manic depression; it varies from person to person. Stressful life events such as losing your job, divorce or bereavement can trigger manic depression in some people. For other people, the trigger may be psychological factors such as chronic anxiety or depression, childhood rejection or family background. It is also thought that some people may have a genetic predisposition towards manic depression.

How common is manic depression?

Manic depression can affect anyone at any time. It can occur in people from all backgrounds, any occupation, and at any time of life. It is equally common in men and women. Around one in 100 in Britain are diagnosed as having manic depression.

What treatments are available?

Most people diagnosed with manic depression are referred to see a psychiatrist. The psychiatrist will conduct an in-depth assessment of your treatment and support needs. The treatments for manic depression are designed to stabilise your mood and prevent the severe swings.

Mood-stabilising drugs

These drugs are not a cure for manic depression, but they can be an effective treatment for the condition. The drugs are designed to combat the extreme mood swings that are characteristic of manic depression. People starting a course of mood-stabilising drugs should be aware that this is usually a long-term treatment rather than a quick fix cure. There are a number of side-effects associated with these drugs, and you may need regular blood tests to ensure that the drug does not reach toxic levels in your blood.

Anti-psychotic drugs

These drugs, also known as major tranquillisers, are sometimes used to treat people during periods of mania. They have a sedative effect and aim to relieve the distressing symptoms associated with manic states. These are powerful drugs that can cause unwanted side-effects. If you are concerned about any side-effects you may be experiencing, it is a good idea to talk these over with your doctor or psychiatrist.

Admission to hospital

If you are very distressed or in an acute state of mania, your doctor may feel that hospital admission offers the best treatment options for you. Hospital can provide a safe environment in which you can be assessed and treated more effectively than if you were at home. Your doctor will normally seek your consent for you to be voluntarily admitted to hospital. However, if your mental state is such that the doctor feels you may be a risk to yourself or others, then you can be admitted to hospital compulsorily under the Mental Health Act 1983.

Crisis services

In some parts of the country, but by no means all, a variety of crisis services have been developed to provide an alternative to hospital admission for some people. Some crisis services provide short-term supported accommodation, but most provide services that enable people to stay in their own homes with regular support.

People diagnosed with manic depression tend to experience mood swings from periods of severe depression to periods of elation known as mania

---

Which treatment may be right for me?

Individuals respond to different treatments in different ways. What works well for one person may not be effective for another. Speaking to your doctor will help you weigh up the pros and cons of the different treatments available. Your doctor should be able to provide you with information on how treatments work, how effective they are, and what side-effects you may experience. Drug treatment may be extremely effective for some people, others may find talking treatments the best option. Others may find a combination of drug treatment and talking treatments works best for them.

What can I do to help myself?

There are many ways in which you can help yourself cope with manic depression. It is important that you come to understand the nature of your illness, its causes and symptoms.

If you can recognise the early signs of a relapse or deterioration in your mental health, you can seek help and treatment before your condition worsens.

When you are feeling depressed, it can be difficult to see beyond the day-to-day problems in life. It can be very difficult finding the energy and motivation to actively try and help yourself. On the other hand, when you are in a manic phase, you may lose insight into the illness and believe that you do not need any support. However, if you are able to take an active part in your treatment it should help your situation to improve.

Self-help groups

Many people find it helpful to meet other people in a similar position. It can be very useful to share experiences with those who may be going through the same thing as you. There are opportunities for mutual support, and you may get ideas of what things other people have found helpful. Above all, it is an opportunity to help you realise that you are not alone in how you are feeling.

Fighting negative attitudes

Depression can cause people to sink into a cycle of negative thinking. The more depressed you become, the less you are able to find the motivation to fight the depression. It can be extremely helpful if you are able to recognise patterns of negative thinking, challenge these yourself, and try and replace them with more positive, constructive thoughts.

Physical activity

Although it may be difficult finding the motivation to exercise, it can be very therapeutic to take part in physical activities. Jogging, swimming, sports, even brisk walking can stimulate production of chemicals in the brain called endorphins. These endorphins can help lift your mood, give you more energy and make you feel better.

Care for yourself

When you are feeling depressed it is extremely important that you care for yourself. Many depressed people

lose the motivation to look after themselves properly. You will feel better if you are able to eat properly, pay attention to your physical appearance, and don't abuse alcohol or drugs. Be kind to yourself, allow yourself treats, and try not to cut yourself off from other people.

Complementary therapies

Some people find non-medical treatments helpful. However, it is important that you discuss such treatments with your doctor first in case of any interaction with any treatment they have prescribed. Massage can help to alleviate stress and make you feel better. Some people benefit from meditation, yoga, homeopathy and acupuncture. You may find creative therapies such as art and poetry can help channel energies.

What can friends and family do to help?

Supporting a friend with manic depression can be frustrating and hard work. However, it can also be immensely satisfying and an opportunity to build a closer relationship. In depressive phases people can withdraw from social situations and relationships and be reluctant to confide in people and ask for help and support. Friends and relatives can be of great help, providing emotional and practical help and encouraging people to seek appropriate support and treatment. Friends and family can become involved in treatment plans and, above all, make the person feel wanted, needed and loved.

■ The above information is re-printed with kind permission from SANE. Visit www.sane.org.uk for more information.

© SANE

Myths and misconceptions about depression

Information from the World Health Organization

In spite of depression being a common illness, many myths and misconceptions are associated with it. Partly, the stigma attached to mental disorders, including depression, is responsible for some of these misconceptions. Such a stigma prejudices the public against people with depression. Attitudes like 'they are unpredictable; they talk and express ideas in a weird manner; they are themselves to blame; they will not recover or improve even if treated', are still widely prevalent. Also, there is inadequate understanding among general practitioners and primary health care physicians regarding appropriate diagnosis and treatment of depression. For these reasons, a large number of persons suffering from depression do not seek help for treatment.

Depression is like any other medical illness. It is caused by the interaction of biological and environmental influences

---

Myth: depression is a problem of the western industrialized world and not of developing countries.
Fact: depression affects all people in all cultures across the world. However, in some countries 'sadness', particularly in old age, is considered 'normal' and not a disease to be treated by a doctor.

Myth: depression is due to the influence of witchcraft, magic or sorcery.
Fact: depression is like any other medical illness. It is caused by the interaction of biological and environmental influences, and manifests in psychological and physical symptoms.

Myth: even if depression is an illness, what can we do about it? We cannot treat it the way other diseases can be treated.
Fact: depression is a treatable disorder. There are many drugs available even in developing countries which are effective and affordable.

Myth: spending scarce resources for treating depression is wasteful expenditure when there are so many other communicable and non-communicable diseases needing attention and which are still not under control in developing countries.
Fact: depression causes considerable suffering among patients worldwide. The burden caused by psychiatric disorders has been underestimated in the past. At present, out of the 10 leading causes of suffering worldwide, five are psychiatric conditions, including depression. By 2020, depression will become the second largest cause of suffering – next only to heart disease.

Myth: there are not enough, and there never will be enough, trained psychiatrists in developing countries to look after all the cases of depression. The situation is hopeless and will never improve.
Fact: the number of psychiatrists is gradually increasing in the developing countries. Moreover, all cases of depression do not have to be treated by psychiatrists. General practitioners and primary health care physicians can satisfactorily treat this illness with some training.

Myth: depression is one's own creation.
Fact: this is completely false. The sufferers cannot be blamed for the illness.

Myth: today's competitive world predisposes a person to depression.

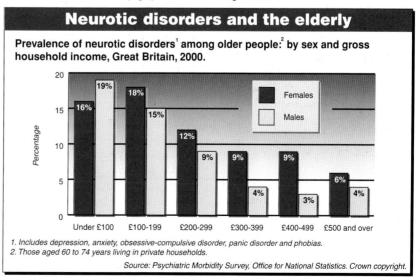

Neurotic disorders and the elderly

Prevalence of neurotic disorders[1] among older people:[2] by sex and gross household income, Great Britain, 2000.

Females
Males

Under £100: Females 16%, Males 19%
£100-199: Females 18%, Males 15%
£200-299: Females 12%, Males 9%
£300-399: Females 9%, Males 4%
£400-499: Females 9%, Males 3%
£500 and over: Females 6%, Males 4%

1. Includes depression, anxiety, obsessive-compulsive disorder, panic disorder and phobias.
2. Those aged 60 to 74 years living in private households.

Source: Psychiatric Morbidity Survey, Office for National Statistics. Crown copyright.

Fact: yes, the world today is very competitive. This may lead to some anxiety and business loss can lead to a person being temporarily sad. However, a person should be able to handle such situations in daily life.

Myth: if a person is depressed, there has to be an external factor bothering him.
Fact: external factors are not always necessary to make a person depressed. It is now known that chemical changes in the brain can lead to depression without any external precipitating factor.

Myth: once depressed, a person remains depressed throughout his/her life.
Fact: in most cases, depression lasts for a limited period. Adequate treatment leads to complete resolution of the symptoms and the person can return to a normal state of activity and health.

Myth: there is no need to go to a medical doctor for treatment. One can cure depression by willpower, a holiday, or at times by taking a peg or two of alcohol to lift one's spirits.
Fact: many communities continue to believe in such home remedies. Willpower cannot cure depression. A depressed person experiencing lack of pleasure in his surroundings will not enjoy his holidays either. Alcohol may worsen the depression. Depression should be treated with prescribed medicines and social support of the family and community.

Myth: drugs used for treating depressions are addictive.
Fact: drugs used for treating depression are not addictive or habit forming. When depression is in remission, the drugs can be slowly tapered off and stopped.

Myth: when a depressed person expresses suicidal ideas, he does not mean to act upon them.
Fact: suicide is a major risk during the course of depression. The individual usually gives an indication of his suicidal intention before attempting suicide and this must be taken very seriously.

Myth: if an individual is suspected to be harbouring suicidal ideas, one should not talk about depression, death or suicide.
Fact: if the discussion about suicide is done sympathetically and tactfully, it gives an opportunity to the individual to express his/her ideas and feelings clearly and to receive appropriate care. In most cases, this prevents suicide.

Myth: a depressed person should be in a sheltered, protected environment for the rest of his/her life.
Fact: once treated successfully, the person returns to his/her normal self, and can resume all personal, social and occupational activities.

Myth: if you have everything in life, all material comforts, you cannot suffer from depression.
Fact: though low socio-economic status may be a contributing factor for depression, it can affect people across all socio-economic levels. Many rich and famous people have been known to have suffered from depression.

■ The above information is reprinted with kind permission from the World Health Organization. Visit www.who.int for more information.
© World Health Organization

Depression in the elderly

Written by Dr Alan Thomas, lecturer and honorary specialist registrar in psychiatry

Depression is the most common mental illness found in old people and the second commonest single underlying cause for all GP consultations for people over 70 years of age.

Symptoms of depression in the elderly

Generally the pattern of depression is similar in elderly people and younger adults and they suffer the same symptoms. However, certain symptoms are more common and some are less common in the elderly than in others.
■ The elderly often do not complain of low mood.
■ Elderly people often experience depression as physical symptoms.

■ Anxiety is a common feature of depression in the elderly.
■ Forgetfulness and confusion occur because of depression in the elderly.

The elderly are less likely to complain of low mood than younger people. When depressed, they may complain of increased aches and pains or other physical symptoms. These can be a way of expressing their depression rather than of the development of any new physical disease.

Many people who are suffering from a depressive illness experience symptoms of anxiety (such as feeling tense, on edge, panicky). The elderly are even more at risk of experiencing these symptoms. The anxiety may be more obvious than a 'low' mood.

Some older people with depression may become confused and forgetful and, in severe cases of depression, they can appear as if they have dementia. This is obviously very frightening for both the person with depression and

others who are looking after them. However, it must be remembered that when the depression is treated these symptoms will go away.

Causes of depression in the elderly

Depression in old age may be triggered by adverse life events including: bereavement; loss of health; threat of bereavement or loss of health in a loved one. Such events are clearly more common experiences for elderly people.

In general, the elderly appear to be better able to cope with such losses than younger people, and so do not develop depression more often. However, as with younger adults, being single and having no close friends makes elderly people more vulnerable to such losses.

More recently, evidence has emerged suggesting that depression occurring for the first time in the elderly can be associated with subtle brain abnormalities, which may be detected by special brain scans. These changes may reflect hidden or undetected vascular (blood vessel) disease in the brain.

Treatment of depression in the elderly

Treatment is broadly similar to treatment in younger adults, and the majority of people respond well to the same antidepressant treatments, which need at least two to four weeks to begin to work. These may be supplemented by supportive counselling by your GP.

People with more severe depression, or those who do not respond to such treatment, may need to be referred to a psychiatrist skilled in treating the elderly. They may respond to another antidepressant or to a combination of antidepressants and other medicines. Electroconvulsive therapy (ECT) can also be very effective in elderly people with severe depression and can be life-transforming.

Depression in old age may be triggered by adverse life events including: bereavement; loss of health; threat of bereavement or loss of health in a loved one

---

Why it is important to recognise depression in the elderly

Too often, depression is dismissed as normal for old people or it is thought it is not severe enough to need antidepressant treatment. Sadly it is often not recognised and so no consideration is given to treatment. This can lead to many months of unnecessary misery and, in some cases, to death from suicide or the physical illnesses, which can be made worse by untreated depression. Since the depression can be expected to respond to treatment, it is tragic if it is not recognised or properly treated.

Recognising depression in the elderly

As elderly people often have physical illnesses, it can be difficult to know whether some of the symptoms (tiredness, poor sleep, poor appetite, weight loss) are due to the illness or depression. In addition, elderly people are less likely to complain of feeling sad. However, the following symptoms may suggest a depressive illness.

- Persistent sadness that does not lift with happy experiences;
- Lack of interest in activities and hobbies that are normally enjoyed;
- A loss of interest in friends and socialising;
- Feelings of guilt and self-blame;
- Marked pessimism about the future;
- Suicidal thoughts and talk of wishing one were dead.

If a few of these have developed over several weeks, then help should be sought, in the first instance, from the family doctor. This is extremely important if the person has expressed any suicidal thoughts.

- The above information is reprinted with kind permission from Net Doctor. Visit www.netdoctor.co.uk for more information.

© *Net Doctor*

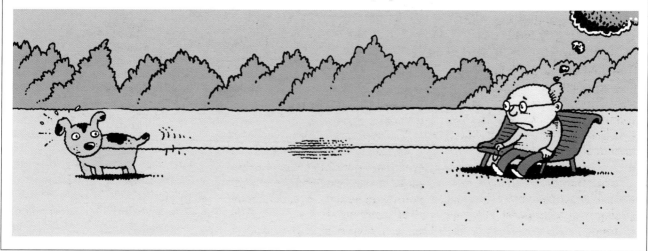

Treating depression

Written by Dr Adrian Lloyd, lecturer and honorary specialist registrar in psychiatry

Introduction

- Throughout this article, 'depression' means depressive illness. This is very different to the normal, brief periods of feeling down that all people occasionally have in response to circumstances in their day-to-day lives.
- Depression is a serious and persistent feeling of sadness that can be accompanied by changes in patterns of sleep, appetite, concentration and energy.
- It can also sometimes involve feelings that life is not worth living or even thoughts of suicide.

Why treat depression?

- It is treatable. A number of effective treatments are available for depression and the right one or the right combination of them can usually be found for each person with the illness.
- It does not just quickly go away on its own, and it can be a disabling and potentially serious condition.
- In a small number of cases it can be fatal because of suicide or because of self-neglect if the sufferer is no longer able to look after his/herself as a result of the illness.

Types of treatment

There are many types of treatment for depression and some of the most frequently used include:

- antidepressant tablets;
- 'talking treatments' such as counselling and various types of psychotherapy;
- mood-stabilising medications;
- support with day-to-day matters while ill or recovering.

Treatments that are used less often, but which can be helpful, especially in depression that is severe, of a

specific type, or has proved difficult to treat, include:

- electroconvulsive therapy (ECT);
- special types of operation (psychosurgery);
- bright light therapy for seasonal affective disorder (SAD).

Lastly, there are potential treatments that are still either experimental, or for which more evidence needs to be found, before they can be considered truly effective and safe:

- herbal remedies (eg St John's wort);
- trans-cranial magnetic stimulation (TMS), which involves applying brief magnetic pulses to the brain. This is done with the patient awake and sitting in

a chair. A doctor holds an electric coil near to the head that emits repeated short magnetic pulses. The procedure is painless. At the present time, TMS is still under investigation as a treatment for depression, however current evidence suggests that it may be as effective as ECT, but safer.

Broadly speaking, treatments for depression can be broken down into two types.

- Firstly, there are those that aim to correct the chemical and biological abnormalities that occur in the illness. These are: antidepressants, mood-stabilising medications, ECT and psychosurgery.
- Secondly, there are the psychological ones – 'talking treatments'. These involve regular appointments to talk to a professional person who is skilled in a particular type of counselling or psychotherapy to help with depression.

The biological and psychological treatments are certainly not mutually exclusive and are often used in combination.

Neither group of treatments or therapies should be considered better than the other. The treatment (or combination of treatments) used should be the one most likely to help a person when all the different factors that have led to their illness are taken into account. This is the reason that approaching a professional is so important in deciding how best to cope with and treat depression.

Antidepressant tablets

There are a number of different groups of these and they include:

- tricyclic antidepressants (TCAs); e.g. amitriptyline, imipramine, lofepramine.

- selective serotonin reputake inhibitors (SSRIs), e.g. fluoxetine, paroxetine, citalopram;
- monoamine-oxidase inhibitors (MAOIs), e.g. moclobemide, phenelzine, tranylcypromine;
- other medicines that do not quite fit neatly into these groups, but that have effects similar to one or more of these groups (e.g. venlafaxine, mirtazapine, reboxetine, trazodone).

For the right person, psychotherapy can be as successful as antidepressant medication in milder depression

---

The oldest antidepressants are the MAOIs and TCAs. The TCAs are still in wide use today and remain effective medicines. The MAOIs require a special diet to avoid unpleasant and potentially serious side-effects, and they can interact with many other medicines. They are therefore generally used only for people whose depression has not responded to other treatments.

The SSRIs are a much newer group of antidepressants, but they have been widely and successfully used for a number of years.

How do they work?
- All antidepressants work by boosting one or more chemicals (called neurotransmitters) in the nervous system. These chemicals may be present in insufficient amounts in depression, resulting in the symptoms of the illness.

Do they work straight away?
- No.
- All antidepressants take a minimum of two weeks (and sometimes up to eight weeks) to start to work, and once they have started working the depression recovers gradually.
- It is vitally important, therefore, that if a person is given antidepressants they should keep taking them regularly, even if

they don't seem to make much difference to begin with.

Are they addictive?
- No.
- Some antidepressants can cause mild unpleasant effects if they are stopped very suddenly, but even these can normally be avoided if the medicine is tailed off over a period of time.

How long should they be taken for?
- A rule of thumb is that antidepressants should be taken for at least six months after the person has recovered. This reduces the risk of the depression coming back again.
- A few people whose depression does return every time they come off antidepressants may need to be on treatment on a long-term basis.

So which is the best type to take?
- There is no evidence to suggest that any one antidepressant or antidepressant group is better than any other in terms of the number of people who will benefit from it. (Generally around two-thirds of people will find that their symptoms improve on any particular medication.)
- But one may be a better choice than another on the grounds of its side effects: for instance a person who finds that their sleep is disturbed may benefit from an antidepressant that is also quite sedative. By contrast someone

who is sleeping reasonably and has to be able to listen out for their children would clearly find this effect a problem, and would be better with a non-sedative medication.
- If an antidepressant from one group does not work very well, then there is a good chance that one from another group may work.

Mood stabilisers
- In depression, these medicines are used to boost the effects of antidepressants.
- The best-known mood stabiliser is lithium. It is also the best-proven one, but one drawback is that regular blood tests are needed to check its level. (Lithium is also used in bipolar affective disorder – 'manic depression'.)
- There are some newer mood stabilisers available now that offer alternatives to lithium.

Electroconvulsive therapy
ECT is a treatment for depression that has been used for many decades, but one that remains controversial.

The facts are:
- it is a very effective treatment for depression – perhaps the single most effective treatment there is;
- it is especially effective for severe depression and depression that has a lot of physical symptoms, such as changes in appetite, sleep and concentration;

- it is as safe as any minor procedure that needs a general anaesthetic;
- it can be life-saving as it can work more quickly than antidepressant medicines;
- there is no good evidence for any permanent damage to the nervous system.

Like all treatments, ECT does have some side effects. These can include:
- headache;
- forgetfulness around the time of treatment.

Psychological treatments

Psychological treatments for depression are many and varied. They range from the psychological support provided when someone has the regular opportunity to talk about their feelings to a professional such as a GP or psychiatrist, right through to very specialised forms of psychotherapy. They include:
- supportive counselling;
- analytic psychotherapy;
- cognitive behavioural therapy (CBT);
- cognitive analytic therapy.

Depression does not just quickly go away on its own, and it can be a disabling and potentially serious condition

There is no evidence to suggest that any one type of therapy is better than any other, but there is reasonably good evidence that, for the right person, psychotherapy can be as successful as antidepressant medication in milder depression.

It can also be used very successfully in conjunction with antidepressants and may add to the effect of the latter.

Having said this, psychotherapy is not the treatment of choice for everyone (in just the same way antidepressants are not the right treatment for everybody). If it is used, the type of psychotherapy that will best suit any individual has to be care-fully considered, highlighting the need for an experienced clinician (e.g. GP, psychiatrist, nurse, psychologist) to be involved in this decision.

Psychotherapy can take place with:
- individuals;
- couples;
- families;
- groups.

It depends on the specific problems and the best ways of approaching them.

Psychotherapy is carried out by a wide range of health professionals including:
- doctors;
- nurses;
- psychologists;
- occupational therapists;
- social workers.

Psychosurgery

Psychosurgery is a form of specialised brain surgery and has been used to treat depressive illness that has failed to respond to long trials of many other treatments. It is performed very infrequently nowadays, and although it does not work for all those who undergo it, it can have beneficial effects.

Social therapies

This term refers to things that can be done to help a person to function as well as possible while they are ill and, crucially in depression, help them to rebuild or strengthen their self-esteem as they recover.

Social therapies can range from planning activities to help someone avoid brooding on problems that may worsen depression, to schemes designed with the help of health and social work staff to help someone build back up to their normal routine.

Depression that is resistant to treatment

Whilst most depressive illnesses will be successfully treated with one of the treatments mentioned, some will not respond as well and may need more specialised combinations of therapies than others. People with these more difficult to treat depressive illnesses should be referred to a psychiatrist.

Where does treatment take place and who arranges it?
- The vast majority of depressive illness is treated by general practitioners (GPs).
- Many GPs have counsellors who can offer supportive sessions.
- Community psychiatric nurses (CPNs) may be available via some GPs or via hospital psychiatry departments.
- GPs will refer patients to psychiatrists and community psychiatric teams (made up typically of psychiatrists, nurses, social workers and psychologists) for further help if needed.
- Most people seeing members of a psychiatric team will have appointments at outpatient clinics or at home.
- Occasionally, if depression is very severe, an admission to hospital may be needed to offer more intensive help.

In summary
- Depression is a readily treatable illness.
- There are many treatments available.
- Even people with the most severe and difficult to treat depressive illnesses can normally be helped.

- The above information is reprinted with kind permission from Net Doctor. Visit www.netdoctor.co.uk for more information.

© Net Doctor

Pills 'are not best way to treat child depression'

Too many children are being prescribed antidepressants when other forms of treatment could be more effective, says the body which advises the government on NHS treatments.

Around half of the 40,000 children and adolescents in the UK on some form of antidepressants do not receive additional back-up counselling and a large proportion should not be on the drugs at all.

The National Institute for Health and Clinical Excellence (NICE), publishing national guidelines yesterday, said doctors should first offer counselling and consider giving children advice on nutrition, exercise and sleep before prescribing powerful antidepressant drugs.

Around half of the 40,000 children and adolescents in the UK on some form of antidepressants do not receive additional back-up counselling

---

Andrew Dillon, Chief Executive of NICE, said: 'This guideline makes it clear that psychological treatments are the most effective way to treat depression in children and young people.

'It's important that children and young people taking antidepressants do not stop taking them abruptly, but we would advise people to talk to their GP at their next regular review about whether a psychological treatment may be a more effective treatment option.'

NICE yesterday advised that children with moderate to severe depression should be offered psychological therapy for at least three months before drugs are considered. It recommended they should be given

By Nic Fleming, Medical Correspondent

antidepressants only in conjunction with psychotherapy.

The institute also called for further training of health care professionals to help them to detect the symptoms of depression.

David Cottrell, Professor Of Child And Adolescent Psychiatry at the University of Leeds, said many children referred were already on some form of medication.

Professor Cottrell, who said his general policy was not to give medication until psychotherapy had been shown to be ineffective, said: 'We do not think that medication should be the first line in treatment. Where psychological therapy has been offered and is not working, medical treatment could be offered as well – the two should interact together.

'Everybody who is working with children needs to get better at detecting depression.'

Professor Cottrell added that teachers, school nurses, social workers and parents should be taught to recognise signs such as irritability, sadness, hopelessness, a lack of interest in things they used to find exciting and withdrawing from friends and family as potential symptoms of depression.

Mental health charities have pointed out that there is a national shortage of trained psychotherapists. Professor Louis Appleby, National Director for Mental Health, welcomed the NICE recommendations as a 'thorough and comprehensive guideline'.

He said: 'Talking therapies are essential components of effective mental health services.

'We know that not everyone who needs treatment is able to access it easily or quickly and expertise and services are not equally distributed around the country.'

The risks

- About 1% of children and 3% of adolescents will suffer from depression in any one year.
- For those with severe depression, the lifetime risk of suicide may be as high as 6% compared to 1.3% in the general population.
- Children with emotional disorders are nearly twice as likely to be living with a lone parent and on low income.
- 10% of children with depression recover in three months.

Professor Appleby said more than £300 million was being invested by the NHS and local authorities into child and adolescent mental health services. 'These resources are going towards providing more staff, better services and faster and easier access to those services around the country.'
28 September 2005

© *Telegraph Group Limited 2006*

Tips on depression and anxiety in children

Information from Parentline Plus

- Even little children get the blues. If your young child doesn't seem happy or is acting differently – try and find out what is upsetting them. If nothing seems to work, check at your child health clinic or contact your GP.
- School-aged children can be really demanding and irritable. Even if they are driving you mad, be patient and say you think they are worried or unhappy. Under all this stroppiness, there may lie lots of hidden anxieties and unhappiness.

Conflict between couples, divorce and separation can cause a lot of anxiety amongst children of any age. Talk them through what is happening and listen to how they feel

---

- Help your kids to get the best out of their school. If they seem low and don't want to go to school, try and find out why and contact the school with your worries.
- Set some ground rules with your teenagers but be prepared to give and take on what they can and can't do. You'll be showing them that you are on their side.
- Don't demand or expect constant love and affection from your children, especially if you are feeling low and your children know it. You could be putting too much of a burden on them and building up layers of guilt and resentment.
- Conflict between couples, divorce and separation can cause a

Parentline plus

lot of anxiety amongst children of any age. Talk them through what is happening and listen to how they feel. That way you'll keep their trust and help them deal with change.
- If your family is going through change, allow yourself and others in the family to have mixed feelings. Different members of your family may feel differently about the same event. Try to let everyone express how they feel, and remember that feelings can change over time.
- Some children like to have other trusted adults they can talk to, a grandparent, aunt or uncle, a teacher, youth worker or family friend. Don't feel threatened if they reach out to someone else. Remembering the fears and anxieties you felt as a child can help you see what your child might be going through and what reassurance they may need.

- Is there something small you can do to make time for yourself? Make a deal with the kids – a trip to the park in exchange for five minutes' peace and quiet. A cup of tea on your own, a hot bath, a chat with your friend.
- You may be feeling isolated, guilty and helpless when trying to comfort your child. You need someone to talk to too – share your feelings with friends, families, partners and other parents – or contact Parentline Plus on 0808 800 2222.
- Trust your own judgement. If you think your child is in need of professional help and you are at all uncomfortable with what is being offered or who is doing the offering, go on looking.
- When trying to get professional help seems an impossible uphill struggle, talking to friends and other members of the family could help you see other ways to ask for help and how you can get heard.

- The above information is reprinted with kind permission from Parentline Plus. Visit www.parentlineplus.org.uk for more information.

© Parentline Plus

Introduction to talking therapies

Information from the Manic Depression Fellowship

What are they?

Talking therapies involve talking and listening. Most of us want somebody to talk to, who listens and accepts us, especially when we are going through a bad time. Sometimes it is easier to talk to a stranger than to relatives or friends.

Most of us want somebody to talk to, who listens and accepts us, especially when we are going through a bad time. Sometimes it is easier to talk to a stranger than to relatives or friends

Some therapists will aim to find the root cause of your problem and help you deal with this, some will help you change your behaviour or negative thoughts, while others simply aim to support you. Therapists are trained to listen and to help you find your own answers, without judging you. Research shows that it is more important how do you get on with the individual therapist than the type of therapy you get. If you can work well together it is more likely to work for you.

People go for talking therapies for a whole range of reasons. Some people may find help and support during a crisis or difficult patch, others find it more helpful to talk after the crisis has passed. In any case it is more likely to help if you want to explore your feelings and change your behaviour.

Talking therapies do not offer magical solutions, it can be hard work and progress can be slow or painful. There are many kinds of therapy

and therapists have different kinds of training. Research shows that it is more important how do you get on with the individual therapist than the type of therapy you get. If you can work well together it is more likely to work for you.

You may want a therapist with a similar background or culture, or you might prefer a female or male therapist. At present, most therapists and counsellors are white and middle class. Your GP should take your preferences into account when arranging your treatment, but you may have a limited choice on the NHS in your area. Talking therapies are also available from voluntary organisations, groups run by and for people from black and minority ethnic communities, women's organisations and groups for people with specific issues.

Who are they for?

Talking therapies are for all sorts of people. Your GP should discuss with you the options regardless of your background or your particular difficulty.

If you see your GP or a psychiatrist for an emotional or mental health problem you may be prescribed drugs such as antidepressants to help with the symptoms. But people often say they would like talking therapy as well as, or instead of, drugs. There is a stigma around talking therapy, and some people feel it is a sign of weakness to go for this type of help. Seeing a therapist doesn't mean you are self-indulgent or going mad.

You may ask your GP for talking therapy regardless of any diagnosis you have been given or any medication you are on. Say if you want it instead of drugs, or if you want to try a combination of drugs and therapy. Most therapists will be happy to work with you while on medication. There is no reason why they shouldn't be used together, in some cases even working better than each on their own.

There is a stigma around talking therapy, and some people feel it is a sign of weakness to go for this type of help. Seeing a therapist doesn't mean you are self-indulgent or going mad.

How and when can I get it?

Talking therapies are available free in the NHS, but what it is available will vary from place to place. There will often be a waiting list. The first step is to see your GP, you will usually need a referral letter to a NHS counsellor, psychologist, psychotherapist or psychiatrist.

GPs vary in their approach to and knowledge about mental health problems, and that can affect whether or not you are offered talking therapies and what type.

If you feel the therapy or therapist is not right for you, or that you need more sessions, you should go back to your GP and ask for another referral.

If your GP is unwilling to refer you for talking therapy, you may have to find out yourself what is available in your area and push hard to get it. If you find another GP who is willing to do it, you may consider changing.

Your first appointment will be for an assessment and you may have to wait after that for treatment. If you are refused, ask for an explanation. Your GP may be able to refer you to another service.

If you are in a long waiting list, think about other options. Your GP may refer you to a local voluntary organisation for counselling or you can approach them yourself. They may ask you for a donation, but no one is turn down for not being able to pay. Some of these organisations are focused on a specific problem (bereavement, eating disorders, etc.).

Private therapists can be expensive, but some will offer a sliding scale based on your income. Talk to several before you decide which one is right for you. Make sure they are members of a recognised professional body such as the UK Council of Psychotherapy or the British Association for Counselling and Psychotherapy.

Many organisations run support groups and self-help networks where you can meet people who have similar experiences.

■ The above information is reprinted with kind permission from the Manic Depression Fellowship. Visit www.mdf.org.uk for more information.

End of the 'prozac nation'

More counselling, more therapy, less medication to treat depression

People suffering from depression will be able to have better access to counselling and talking therapies under a major new programme announced today by Health Secretary, Patricia Hewitt.

At the moment many people with mild to moderate depression find it difficult to access talking therapies, with services patchily spread across the country

At the moment many people with mild to moderate depression find it difficult to access talking therapies, with services patchily spread across the country. This is despite clinical evidence showing that better access to therapies such as cognitive behavioural therapy (CBT) can help cure depression and reduce time off work due to ill-health. Patients also prefer to receive talking therapies rather than medication.

The programme, announced today by Patricia Hewitt in a speech to the National Mental Health Partnership Conference, consists of two demonstration sites in Doncaster and Newham, which will be linked to a regional network of local improvement programmes. The two demonstration sites will bring together key programmes in the NHS, voluntary sector and local employers to test various models that can be implemented nationally.

Announcing the launch of the programme today, Miss Hewitt said: 'Millions of people suffer from mild to moderate mental health problems, and treating them takes up about a third of GPs' time. Too many people are prescribed medication as a quick fix solution, but talking therapies

work equally well and patients prefer to receive them.

'We know that people in work have better health than those out of work and the *Choosing Health* White Paper made clear that work matters – it can improve your mental and physical health, reduce health inequalities and improve life chances for people and their families.

About one in three of the 1.3 million people claiming long-term incapacity benefit in the UK have a mental health problem, mostly mild to moderate depression

---

'I hope that these pilot sites will provide real, tangible evidence of the effectiveness of investing in talking therapies. They will help break the cycle of deprivation, where poor health leads to unemployment and wasted lives as people fail to reach their full potential.'

Rethink Chief Executive Cliff Prior said: 'This could be the beginning of a dramatic advance in mental health. We know from our members that there is a huge demand for talking therapies. We also know that there is already a strong evidence base to support these types of interventions. We hope that the pilot sites will report quickly and positively so that this initiative can become a full national programme available to everyone who needs it.'

Paul Farmer, Chief Executive of Mind, said: 'Mind has long been campaigning for a wider choice of therapies, including talking therapies, to be readily available on the NHS for all who need them. We hope that these pilot schemes will be a first step towards making this a reality, and look forward to the scheme's extension to cover the whole population.

'We are delighted to finally see delivery of pilot schemes for these urgently needed alternative treatments to medication, now advocated by several NICE guide-

lines as frontline treatments. Giving people the chance to learn coping strategies and self-management techniques can help reduce the risk of mental health problems returning later on.'

Sainsbury Centre for Mental Health Chief Executive Angela Greatley said: 'People with depression and anxiety have for too long been offered little more than medication. For a significant minority, this is not enough to help them to recover. As a result, many lose their jobs, drop out of education or see their relationships break down. Waiting times for psychological therapies are long, despite the mass of evidence about their benefits for many people. Today's announcement should be the beginning of a new approach that ensures timely access to effective treatment and practical support, with real choices and care close to home.'

Notes

1. Improving access to talking therapies has the potential to save the economy millions of pounds by helping people with mild to moderate depression to get back into employment and off incapacity benefit. About one in three of the 1.3 million people claiming long-term incapacity benefit in the UK have a mental health problem, mostly mild to moderate depression.

2. The pilots will provide real evidence of the benefits that can be gained from increasing access to psychological therapies, both to the individual and to the local economy. They have been given £3.7 million funding over two years from the Department of Health.

The two sites have been chosen because they serve very different demographics with different health needs, and they offer different treatment models such as community-based, voluntary sector-led, or employer-led.

Local people will benefits from the pilots by having:

- access to coping strategies and support as an alternative to taking sick leave from work due to depression;
- better support in the workplace from occupational health;
- retaining employment, even where the individual may suffer from stress, anxiety or depression;
- enabling people on benefits to return to work more quickly;
- more choice over their care and treatment.

12 May 2006

■ The above information is reprinted with kind permission from the Department of Health. Visit www.dh.gov.uk for more information.

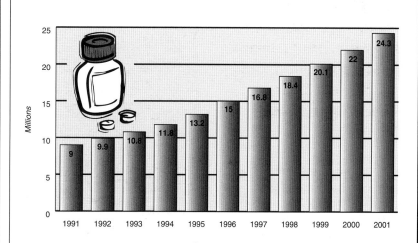

Prescriptions for antidepressant drugs

Number of prescription items for antidepressant drugs[1], by year, England.

1. Dispensed in the community. See Appendix, Part 7: Prescription Cost Analysis System. Antidepressants are defined as those drugs within the British National Formulary (BNF) section 4.3, antidepressant drugs.

Source: Department of Health. Crown copyright.

Quick guide to antidepressants

Information from SANE

How effective are antidepressant drugs?

Antidepressants can be very effective. They are generally non-addictive and do not lose effectiveness with prolonged use. Three people out of four respond to antidepressants. Of those that don't, about half will respond to a different medicine.

How long does it take for antidepressants to work?

Most people with depression will respond to treatment after two weeks but in some people, it can take up to four weeks. All drugs work at the same speed.

How long will I need treatment?

Studies have shown that continuing antidepressants for at least six months after a first episode reduces the risk of further episodes. However, long-term studies of up to 10 years have shown that half to three-quarters of all those who had suffered a depressive disorder suffered a relapse. Long-term treatment of up to five years may be necessary for some people.

Drug choice

Because all antidepressants are equally effective, doctors choose medication according to side-effects and how well they mix with other medicines taken. It may take one or two attempts before a suitable medication is found.

Stopping antidepressant drugs

When taken for six weeks or longer, antidepressants should not be stopped suddenly as they have the potential to cause withdrawal symptoms. These can include dizziness, anxiety and agitation, insomnia, flu-like symptoms, diarrhoea, nausea and low mood.

What are the side effects of antidepressants?

Unfortunately all the antidepressants may cause side-effects. Most of the common side-effects usually wear off with time (as the body gets more used to the drug). If a particular side-effect is still troublesome after a few weeks, there is usually an alternative drug you can try.

Depression is thought to be caused by a reduction in the level of certain chemicals in the brain (called neurotransmitters). These affect mood by stimulating brain cells

---

How do antidepressants work?

Depression is thought to be caused by a reduction in the level of certain chemicals in the brain (called neurotransmitters). These affect mood by stimulating brain cells. Antidepressants increase the level of certain important neurotransmitters.

Types of antidepressants

Tricyclics

Tricyclics act by blocking the re-uptake of the neurotransmitters serotonin and noradrenaline, thereby increasing levels at their receptors.

Selective serotonin re-uptake inhibitors (SSRIs)

SSRI's act by blocking the re-uptake of only one neurotransmitter, serotonin.

Monoamine-oxidase inhibitors (MAOIs)

MAOIs act by blocking the breakdown of excitatory neuro-transmitters, mainly serotonin and noradrenaline.

■ The above information is re-printed with kind permission from SANE. Visit www.sane.org.uk for more information.

© SANE

www.independence.co.uk

32

Psychotherapy for all?

LSE Depression Report urges choice of psychological therapy for all

The LSE's Depression Report, published on Monday 19 June, urges that psychological therapy should be made available to all people suffering from depression, chronic anxiety and schizophrenia. This is what the guidelines from the National Institute for Health and Clinical Excellence (NICE) prescribe, but they are not currently being implemented because the therapy services are not there.

One in six of all people suffer from depression or chronic anxiety, which affects one in three of all families

According to the authors of the report, the Centre for Economic Performance's Mental Health Policy Group, led by Lord Professor Richard Layard, there should be a proper psychological therapy service in every part of the country by 2013. Such a service would pay for itself in the reduced expenditure on incapacity benefits from people being able to go back to work.

The report reveals the following striking facts.

- There are more mentally-ill people on incapacity benefits than

the total number of unemployed people on benefit.
- One in six of all people suffer from depression or chronic anxiety, which affects one in three of all families.
- Only a quarter of those who are ill are receiving any treatment – in most cases, medication.
- Modern evidence-based psychological therapy is as effective as medication and is preferred by the majority of patients.
- In most areas, waiting lists are over nine months, if therapy is available at all.
- A course of therapy costs £750 and pays for itself in money saved on incapacity benefits and lost tax receipts.
- We can therefore provide a service in every area at no net cost. This would require 10,000 therapists and 250 local services, with 40 new services opened each year till 2013. With proper leadership from the Centre and protected funding, this is totally feasible.

The report has the support of the Royal College of General

Practitioners, as well as leading mental health charities – Mind, Rethink, Sane, the Mental Health Foundation and the Sainsbury Centre for Mental Health.

The Chairman of the Royal College of General Practitioners, Professor Mayur Lakhani, said: 'GPs tell me all the time just how hard it is to get talking therapies for their patients. I welcome this important proposal, which, if implemented, could transform the care of thousands of patients with anxiety and depression.'
19 June 2006

- The above information is reprinted with kind permission from the Centre for Economic Performance at the London School of Economics. Visit www.lse.ac.uk for more information.

© *Centre for Economic Performance/LSE*

Electroconvulsive therapy

A series of short, sharp shocks? ECT doesn't evoke the nicest of images. TheSite takes a look at this controversial treatment

Short sharp shock

Made famous by its mention in Sylvia Plath's *The Bell Jar*, ECT doesn't evoke the nicest of images. It is estimated that in Britain 138,000 ECT sessions are carried out each year.

Why have ECT?

- ECT is usually given to people with severe depression that hasn't responded to other forms of treatment such as antidepressants.
- However, it is sometimes used for those with a diagnosis of bipolar affective disorder (manic depression) or schizophrenia.

ECT is a psychiatric treatment in which a brief electrical stimulus is given to the brain via electrodes placed on the temples

---

- It is usually only given after the risks have been explained and with the person's consent, or in the extreme case when the person's life is at risk, for example when they are unable to eat or drink.

What does the treatment involve?

ECT is a psychiatric treatment in which a brief electrical stimulus is given to the brain via electrodes placed on the temples. The electrical charge lasts between one to four seconds, and causes a type of epileptic seizure.

How often do you need to have ECT?

Most patients are given a course of between six and 12 ECT sessions at a rate of one a day, three times a week. In severe cases, ECT can be given without the patient's consent under UK legislation.

Why the controversy?

Controversy surrounds the safety, ethics and necessity of ECT. In particular, some people who use mental health services believe that the side-effects can be quite severe and that they have had ECT administered to them either against their will, or without their knowledge (in cases where people are so depressed that they are unaware of what is going on around them).

The UK Advocacy Network's survey of people who had received ECT treatment found that 30% of people who had received ECT found it helpful or very helpful, while more than 50% found it unhelpful or damaging. Specific complaints include:

- poor standards: inspectors appointed by the Royal College of Psychiatrists found that many ECT clinics did not follow safe and humane practices;

- limited benefits: clinical trials do not demonstrate long-lasting benefits of ECT beyond a few weeks. However, doctors argue that it is sometimes life-saving to lift a person quickly out of a life-threatening depression, and allow the possibility that other therapies, or the healing effects of time, can begin to work. There have also been cases of immediate recovery following ECT;

- memory loss: the UK Advocacy Network's survey of people who had received ECT treatment found that 73% of respondents reported memory loss (not all short-term);

- psychological adverse affects: some people say they find ECT extremely upsetting, reasons for this include feelings of fear, shame and humiliation, worthlessness and helplessness, and a sense of having been abused and assaulted;

- deaths caused by ECT: some reports claim that there as many as 4.5 deaths per 10,000 ECT patients.

- The above information is reprinted with kind permission from TheSite.org. Visit www.thesite.org for more information.

© *TheSite.org*

Responding to depression

Electric shock treatment 'best response' to depression

Drugs and electric shock therapy are still the best way to treat depression, a paper in *The Lancet* medical journal says today, rejecting NHS guidance that people do better and are safer on talking therapies.

Klaus Ebmeier from Edinburgh University and colleagues dismiss recommendations to doctors from the National Institute for Health and Clinical Excellence (NICE) as in effect pandering to public opinion.

Confidence has been lost in the modern antidepressants known as SSRIs (selective serotonin re-uptake inhibitors) because of publicity around revelations that they can cause suicidal feelings in children, they say.

> ### Confidence has been lost in the modern antidepressants known as SSRIs because of publicity around revelations that they can cause suicidal feelings in children

'The NICE recommendations are representative of a trend in public perception, which seems to run ahead of contemporary clinical practice,' they write. While effectiveness has usually been the main criterion for making treatment recommendations in the past, 'risks of side effects and patients' choice are increasingly taking their place next to treatment effectiveness.'

The authors say that NICE went 'well beyond guidelines published by the American Psychiatric Association' and that there are problems with implementing the recommendations.

Reviewing published studies on drugs and other therapies, they

By Sarah Boseley, Health Editor

conclude that antidepressants and ECT (electroconvulsive therapy) are the best treatments.

But Tim Kendall, joint director of the National Collaborating Centre for Mental Health, which produced the guidelines for NICE, says it is not possible to get a complete picture of the risks and benefits of antidepressants because drug companies have published only a limited number of usually positive trials.

When they were preparing the NICE guidelines, his team had access to only a fraction of the studies that were done – for example, only half of the studies of drugs for obsessive compulsive disorders. Where SSRIs have an effect it is small, he said. A study published in the *American Journal of Psychiatry* found that less than one in three patients benefited from one of the drugs, called citalopram.

ECT is still regularly used by psychiatrists in spite of a vocal lobby, including some former patients, against it. In the first three months of 1999, according to an assessment report produced by NICE, ECT was used on 2,835 patients in England.

The main objection is loss of memory, but that can be temporary, say the authors of the review. However, the effects of ECT are short-lived, so patients are likely to need drug treatment later.

13 January 2006

Young people and mental health

Prevalence of mental health disorders in boys and girls in 2004.

Legend:
- 5 to 10-year-old boys
- 11 to 16-year-old boys
- 5 to 10-year-old girls
- 11 to 16-year-old girls

Disorder	5 to 10-year-old boys	11 to 16-year-old boys	5 to 10-year-old girls	11 to 16-year-old girls
Conduct disorder	6.9%	8.1%	2.8%	5.1%
Hyperkinetic disorder	2.7%	2.4%	0.4%	0.4%
Emotional disorder	2.2%	4.0%	2.5%	6.1%
Less common disorders	2.2%	1.6%	0.4%	1.1%
Any disorder	10.2%	12.6%	5.1%	10.3%

Percentage

Source: Office for National Statistics (2005), 'Mental health of children and young people in Great Britain, 2004'. London: HMSO. Crown copyright.

Cheers?

Self-medication with alcohol is widespread, says new mental health report

The Mental Health Foundation has today released *Cheers?* – a new research report outlining the relationship between alcohol and mental health.

The report shows evidence that many adults in the UK are using alcohol to deal with feelings of stress, anxiety and depression, and excessive drinking increases vulnerability to a range of mental health problems.

National opinion poll research carried out to identify reasons for drinking shows that people say alcohol makes them feel:

- relaxed (77 per cent);
- happy (63 per cent);
- more able to fit in socially (44 per cent);
- more confident (41 per cent).

The results also reveal that drinking alcohol makes people:

- feel less anxious (40 per cent);
- less depressed (26 per cent);
- more able to forget their problems (30 per cent).

This is consistent with the theory that people use alcohol to cope with feelings of stress, anxiety and depression

Evidence outlined in the *Cheers?* report also shows that people who drink high volumes of alcohol are vulnerable to mental ill-health. Over the last 50 years, alcohol consumption has doubled in the UK, mirroring an increase in the number of people experiencing mental ill-health.

Regular drinking changes the chemistry of the brain and depletes the neurotransmitters the brain needs to prevent anxiety and depression naturally. According to the World Health Organization, enough evidence exists to show alcohol can contribute to depression.

According to the Mental Health Foundation, physical health concerns related to increasing alcohol consumption are being reflected in government policy developments, yet very little attention has been given to the links between alcohol and mental health, with little debate about why people drink alcohol.

Dr Andrew McCulloch, Chief Executive of the Mental Health Foundation, said:

'The research confirms our worries that people are drinking to cope with emotions and situations they can't otherwise manage, to deal with feelings of anxiety and depression.

Over the last 50 years, alcohol consumption has doubled in the UK

'Drinking alcohol is a very common and accepted way of coping – our culture allows us to use alcohol for "medicinal purposes" or "Dutch courage" from an early age. But using alcohol to deal with anxiety and depression doesn't work as alcohol can weaken the neurotransmitters that the brain needs to reduce anxiety and depressive thoughts. This is why lots of people feel low when they have a hangover.'

The Mental Health Foundation believes that the public has a right to information about the hazardous effects that alcohol misuse can have on their mental as well as physical health. The report makes a number of government policy recommendations.

Key facts

- The UK ranks 22 out of 185 countries in alcohol consumption.
- 38 per cent of men and 16 per cent of women drink above recommended limits and can be classed as having an alcohol use disorder.
- 1.1 million people in the UK are dependent on alcohol.
- 70 per cent of men who commit suicide have drunk alcohol before doing so.
- Almost one-third of suicides amongst young people are committed when a young person is intoxicated.

Report national opinion poll findings

- 88 per cent say they would find it difficult to give up alcohol completely.
- 77 per cent say alcohol makes them feel relaxed.

- 63 per cent say alcohol makes them feel happy.
- 51 per cent say alcohol makes them feel less inhibited.

As more alcohol enters the bloodstream, the areas of the brain associated with emotions and movement are affected

---

- 41 per cent say alcohol makes them feel more confident.
- 44 per cent say alcohol makes them able to fit in socially.

The science – how alcohol affects the mind and body

Alcohol is a toxic substance. The initial impact of a drink – the 'winding down' or relaxing feeling – is a reflection of immediate chemical changes occurring in the brain's nerve cells in response to alcohol. As more alcohol is consumed, increasingly sensitive parts of the brain become affected and behaviour changes accordingly.

The first drink for many people (although not all) depresses the parts of the brain that are associated

- 40 per cent say alcohol makes them feel less anxious.
- 31 per cent say alcohol makes them able to make friends more easily.

with inhibition, increasing talking and self-confidence and reducing social anxiety. As more alcohol enters the bloodstream, the areas of the brain associated with emotions and movement are affected, often resulting in exaggerated states of emotion such as anger, withdrawal, depression or aggressiveness, and uncoordinated muscle movements. Alcohol then depresses the nerve centres in the area that controls sexual arousal (which increases) and performance (which doesn't).
18 April 2006

- The above information is re-printed with kind permission from the Mental Health Foundation. Visit www.mentalhealth.org.uk for more.
© Mental Health Foundation

The lowdown: seasonal affective disorder (SAD)

An expert guide to the disorder that affects about half a million people in the UK

Light therapy

Description

Opinion is divided on what causes SAD, but instances increase dramatically around the time the clocks change and the daylight hours become fewer. One of the most popular and effective treatments is light-box therapy, which involves wearing a light visor for up to an hour a day or sitting near a light box.

St John's Wort (or Hypericum) is a yellow-flowered plant that has been used for centuries as a mild antidepressant

---

Where to get it

There are many different kinds of light box and, since they are not available on the NHS, they are expensive – at least £200. However, most dealers offer a 30-day trial period or rental deals. Information

---

By Phil Maynard

---

and a range of light boxes and visas can be found at www.outsidein.co.uk (01954 780500).

Effectiveness

Clinical trials and much anecdotal evidence support the manufacturers' claims that light therapy is effective in many cases of moderate SAD. In clinical trials when used between 20 and 60 minutes a day, the majority of sufferers reported an improvement in their condition.

Side-effects

If you have a history of serious eye problems or are using any medication which makes the skin more sensitive to light you should consult a doctor first. Side effects can include headaches and eyestrain. You should only use purpose-built light boxes to minimise risks.

St John's Wort

Description

St John's Wort (or Hypericum) is a yellow-flowered plant that has

been used for centuries as a mild antidepressant. Exactly how this herbal remedy works is still not quite understood, but the chemicals hypericin and hyperforin are believed to be active ingredients.

Where to get it

Unlike conventional antidepressants, St John's Wort is available without prescription in many high-street pharmacists. It comes in capsule form or as a tea. Expect to pay between £5 and £10 for 100 capsules.

Effectiveness

St John's Wort is widely prescribed in Europe for mild depression (including SAD) and is thought to be effective. However, research is ongoing and conclusive evidence has yet to be published. In moderate and severe depression, St John's Wort has had little or no effect in clinical trials.

Side effects

St John's Wort is not completely safe just because it is 'natural'. If you are taking medication for any other condition it is important to check with a doctor first. It also interferes with the oral contraceptive pill. Side-effects include dry mouth, nausea, diarrhoea, sensitivity to sunlight, and fatigue.

Cognitive behavioural therapy
Description
Cognitive behavioural therapy (CBT) is a psychological treatment that assumes that behavioural and emotional reactions are learned over a long period. A cognitive therapist will seek to identify the source of emotional problems and develop techniques to overcome them.
Where to get it
There is a chronic shortage of NHS cognitive therapists and it is often difficult to find private ones. Expect to pay anywhere between £50 and £90 for a session. Contact the British Association for Behavioural and Cognitive Psychotherapists (01254 875277); www.babcp.org.uk.
Effectiveness
There is evidence to suggest that cognitive and behavioural therapies can be very effective in treating a range of psychological problems, although the jury is still out on its efficacy for SAD specifically. Since it can be used in conjunction with other treatments, it is highly recommended.
Side-effects
Unless you are in the fortunate position of getting CBT on the NHS, it is likely to burn a big hole in your finances.

Antidepressants
Description
For those already on antidepressants and who experience worse depression in the winter months, doctors may increase their medication. Others who do not respond to other treatments such as light therapy may be prescribed selective serotonin re-uptake inhibitors (SSRIs) such as fluoxetine (Prozac).
Where to get it
Antidepressants are available by prescription only and therefore the standard charge applies (£6.40).
Effectiveness
It is difficult to pin down the effectiveness of SAD treatments as the condition often resolves itself when winter turns to spring. However,

clinical trials show that in patients who have not responded to other SAD treatments, antidepressants prior to or during the winter are effective.
Side-effects
The most common side effect of SSRIs is flu-like symptoms upon withdrawal of the drug after treatment. SSRIs are not addictive in the same way as tranquillisers, but many people who follow a long course of medication do become psychologically dependent.

5-HTP
Description
5-Hydroxy-tryptophan (5-HTP) is a chemical compound broken down by the body into serotonin (the hormone often found to be low in people suffering from depression and SAD).
Where to get it
5-HTP is not available on the NHS but many brands can be purchased from alternative health retailers such as Holland & Barrett. Expect to pay between £8 and £12 for a pack of 60 tablets. It also occurs naturally in some foods (e.g. cheese and turkey).

Anyone can improve their health and mood in winter by adopting a healthier lifestyle

---

Effectiveness
The jury is still out on 5-HTP – studies have not yielded definitive results – so the drug is not widely used. But some clinical studies have shown it to have more than a placebo effect. Evidence also suggests that 5-HTP acts as an appetite suppressant (SAD sufferers often eat more during the winter).
Side-effects
Doctors do not usually recommend 5-HTP because it has not yet been shown to be completely safe. However, many alternative therapists encourage its use but warn of side-effects such as nausea and drowsiness. It may interfere with other medicines you are taking, so you should always check with your GP first.

Diet and exercise
Description
By eating the right amounts of the right foods and exercising daily, you can minimise the symptoms of SAD and experience other health benefits. Experts recommend a balanced diet including a daily intake of breads and cereals, fruits and vegetables, dairy products and meat and fish (or their nutritional equivalents).

Where to get it
Anyone can improve their health and mood in winter by adopting a healthier lifestyle. A good way to start is to cut back on stodgy and fatty foods, caffeine, nicotine and alcohol. Drink plenty of water and try to exercise for at least half an hour every day – go for a walk at lunchtime and take the stairs instead of the lift.
Effectiveness
SAD often resolves itself naturally, but by maximising the time you are outside, increasing the amount of exercise taken and eating healthily you can effectively boost energy levels, improve sleeping habits and feel healthier all round.
Side-effects
Don't attempt too much too soon. By exercising a little to begin with then gradually increasing the amount, you are more likely to avoid muscle injury and more likely to enjoy it.
■ Words by Phil Maynard, in consultation with Dr Richard Bowskill, consultant psychiatrist at the Priory in Hove and Daniela Turley, medical herbalist at the Hale Clinic in London.
17 November 2005
© Guardian Newspapers Limited 2006

Quick-fix tips for depression

If you suffer from mild depression or are simply feeling low, self-help methods may help you feel balanced and content once more

Depression Alliance, the UK charity for people affected by depression, have put together these techniques to help alleviate the blues. These should be seen not as alternatives to, but as complementary to, professional treatment.

- Sharing experiences: talking to a positive and supportive friend or relative will help. It will also make you feel less isolated. Remember that depression often affects your self-esteem and makes you feel unloved. This can stop you contacting friends and family, which can leave you even more depressed! Don't get into this vicious circle – ask for, and accept, the love and support of people who care for you. Depression Alliance also provides forums for sharing experiences with people who understand.

- Gathering information: finding out more about depression can reduce the misconceptions, guilt and fear that are often associated with the condition. A wide range of leaflets, videos, and tapes on depression are available from Depression Alliance; you could also look in your local library or on the Internet. Contact Depression Alliance for a useful reading list, which includes books, tapes and websites on depression.

- Relaxation: depression is frequently associated with tension, stress and anxiety. Increasing amounts of evidence show that relaxation is one of the best treatments for depression. There are many ways to relax – yoga, reading, listening to a relaxation tape or going away for a short holiday. Find out what works for you and give yourself time to unwind.

Depression**Alliance**

- Exercise: many people with depression experience a loss of energy and constant feelings of tiredness. Taking some form of gentle exercise will make you feel more positive, releasing endorphins or 'feel good' chemicals. Exercise will also contribute to your overall health, enabling you to better fight off the depression.

- Changes to your diet: depression can affect your appetite, so make sure that you eat regular, appropriate amounts. Missing out valuable nutrients can also make people feel tired and run down, so try to include fresh fruit and vegetables in your diet. Research shows that some essential fatty acids like omega-3 play an important part in fighting depression. Foods that may help include bananas, chillies, oily fish and dark green vegetables.

- Pursuing interests: try to continue with any hobbies or interests you have. It may be difficult while you are depressed, especially if you have difficulty concentrating, but it will help you to feel better.

- Complementary, or 'alternative', treatments can support or, in some cases, even replace conventional treatments for depression. Research on acupuncture, herbal medicines (including St John's Wort), and aromatherapy suggests that these treatments can help to reduce anxiety and alleviate mild depression. You should always talk to your GP before opting for a complementary treatment.

For more information on self-help and where to get support for depression go to www.depressionalliance.org.

- The above information is reprinted with kind permission from Depression Alliance. Visit www.depressionalliance.org for more information.

© *Depression Alliance*

■ The feeling of depression is much more powerful and unpleasant than the short episodes of unhappiness that we all experience from time to time. It goes on for much longer. It can last for months rather than days or weeks. (page 1)

■ Anyone can become depressed, but some of us seem to be more likely to than others. This may be because of the particular make-up of our body, because of experiences early in our life, or both. (page 2)

■ Post-natal depression is a common condition, affecting between 10% and 20% of new mothers. Starting two or three weeks after delivery, it often develops slowly, making it more difficult to diagnose. Often it goes unrecognised by the woman herself, or by her family. (page 4)

■ Depression, anxiety and other forms of mental illness have taken over from unemployment as the greatest social problem in the UK, a health economist has warned. (page 7)

■ Around 15% of the population suffers from depression or anxiety. (page 7)

■ More than a million children are suffering in an epidemic of depression and anxiety, a report has revealed. (page 9)

■ A *Mixmag* magazine survey found that regular ecstasy users are 25% more likely to suffer a mental health disorder than the rest of the population and were twice as likely to have seen a doctor about mental health issues, with half of those being concerned about depression. (page 10)

■ Figures show that mental ill-health is costing the UK almost £100 billion a year. (page 11)

■ Evidence released by the Mental Health Foundation and Sustain reveals that changes to the human diet in the last 50 years or so could be an important factor behind the major rise of mental ill-health in the UK. (page 11)

■ One in six people will have depression at some point in their life. (page 16)

■ Depression is most common in people aged 25 to 44 years. (page 16)

■ More women than men are diagnosed as having seasonal affective disorder. Children and adolescents are also vulnerable. (page 18)

■ Depression affects all people in all cultures across the world. However, in some countries 'sadness', particularly in old age, is considered 'normal' and not a disease to be treated by a doctor. (page 21)

■ At present, out of the 10 leading causes of suffering worldwide, five are psychiatric conditions, including depression. By 2020, depression will become the second largest cause of suffering – next only to heart disease. (page 21)

■ Depression is the most common mental illness found in old people and the second commonest single underlying cause for all GP consultations for people over 70 years of age. (page 22)

■ Around half of the 40,000 children and adolescents in the UK on some form of antidepressants do not receive additional back-up counselling and a large proportion should not be on the drugs at all. (page 27)

■ About 1 per cent of children and 3 per cent of adolescents will suffer from depression in any one year. (page 27)

■ At the moment many people with mild to moderate depression find it difficult to access talking therapies, with services patchily spread across the country. This is despite clinical evidence showing that better access to therapies such as cognitive behavioural therapy (CBT) can help cure depression and reduce time off work due to ill-health. (page 30)

■ Antidepressants can be very effective. They are generally non-addictive and do not lose effectiveness with prolonged use. Three people out of four respond to antidepressants. Of those that don't, about half will respond to a different medicine. (page 32)

■ One in six of all people suffer from depression or chronic anxiety. (page 33)

■ Only a quarter of those who are ill with depression or anxiety are receiving any treatment – in most cases medication. (page 33)

■ Drugs and electric shock therapy are still the best way to treat depression, a paper in *The Lancet* medical journal says, rejecting NHS guidance that people do better and are safer on talking therapies. (page 35)

■ Many adults in the UK are using alcohol to deal with feelings of stress, anxiety and depression, and excessive drinking increases vulnerability to a range of mental health problems. (page 36)

GLOSSARY

5-HTP
5-Hydroxy-tryptophan (5-HTP) is a chemical compound broken down by the body into serotonin (the hormone often found to be low in depression sufferers).

Antidepressant tablets
These include tricyclic antidepressants (TCAs), selective serotonin re-uptake inhibitors (SSRIs) and monoamine oxidase inhibitors (MAOIs). Of these, the SSRIs are a much newer group, but the MAOIs and TCAs have been used widely and successfully for a number of years. Antidepressants work by boosting one or more chemicals (neurotransmitters) in the nervous system, which may be present in insufficient amounts during a depressive illness.

Anti-psychotic drugs
Also known as major tranquillisers, these are sometimes used to treat bipolar affective disorder sufferers during periods of mania. They have a sedative effect and aim to relieve the distressing symptoms associated with manic states.

Bipolar affective disorder
Previously called manic depression, this type of depressive illness is characterised by mood swings where periods of severe depression are balanced by periods of elation and overactivity. This affects about one in 10 people who suffer from depression and tends to run in families.

Cognitive behavioural therapy (CBT)
A psychological treatment that assumes that behavioural and emotional reactions are learned over a long period. A cognitive therapist will seek to identify the source of emotional problems and develop techniques to overcome them.

Depression
Someone is said to be significantly depressed, or suffering from depression, when feelings of sadness or misery don't go away quickly and are so bad that they interfere with everyday life.

Electroconvulsive therapy (ECT)
A treatment for depression which has been used for many decades, but remains controversial, as some people who use mental health services believe the side-effects can be quite severe. It involves a brief electrical stimulus given to the brain via electrodes placed on the temples. It is estimated that in Britain, 138,000 ECT sessions are carried out each year.

Endogenous depression
Not always triggered by an upsetting or stressful event. Sufferers may experience weight change, tiredness, sleeping problems, low mood, poor concentration and low self-esteem.

Light therapy
A treatment for seasonal affective disorder (SAD) which involves wearing a light visor for up to an hour a day or sitting near a light box.

Mood stabilisers
In depression, these drugs are used to boost the affects of antidepressants. The best-known and best-proven mood stabiliser is lithium, which may also be used to treat bipolar affective disorder. However, regular blood tests are needed to check its level.

Post-natal depression
Depression experienced by new mothers. It is not known for certain what causes it, but some experts believe the sudden change in hormones after a baby's birth may be the trigger. It affects at least one in 10 new mothers, although often unrecognised. Symptoms may include panic attacks, sleeping difficulties, overwhelming fear of death and feelings of inadequacy/being unable to cope.

'Prozac nation'
A term coined to describe the UK's increasing dependence on antidepressant drugs such as Prozac.

Psychosurgery
A form of specialised brain surgery for treating depression that has failed to respond to long trials of other treatments. It is used infrequently nowadays.

Reactive depression
Depression triggered by a traumatic, difficult or stressful event, or following a prolonged period of stress. Sufferers may feel low, anxious, irritable or angry.

Seasonal affective disorder (SAD)
A type of depression which generally coincides with the approach of winter and is linked to shortening of daylight hours and lack of sunlight. Roughly 2% of the population of Northern Europe suffer badly.

St John's Wort (Hypericum)
A yellow-flowered plant that has been used for centuries as a mild antidepressant.

Talking therapies
Talking treatments for depression involve talking and listening. Some therapists will aim to find the root cause of a sufferer's problem and help them deal with it, some will help to change behaviour and negative thoughts, while others simply offer support. They are trained to listen without judging.

INDEX

5-HTP and SAD 38

activity as help for depression 3, 39
alcohol
    and depression 2, 3, 36-7
    effects 37
    as self-medication 36-7
    underage drinking 9
Alzheimer's disease, role of diet 12
anti-psychotic drugs 19
antidepressants 24-5, 32
    and adolescents 8, 27
    and children 27
    and postnatal depression 18
    and SAD 38
anxiety in children 28

bipolar affective disorder (manic depression) 2, 4, 10,
    19-20
brain, effects of alcohol 37

causes of depression 2
    in the elderly 23
    manic depression 19
    in people with physical illnesses 6
children
    alcohol and mental health problems 9
    and depression 27-8
    and mental health problems 16
cognitive behavioural therapy and SAD 38
communication, importance of 3, 39
    young people 8
complementary therapies 39
    and manic depression 20
costs
    mental health problems 16
    psychological therapy 7
counselling services 30-31
    postnatal depression 18
criminal activity and mental health problems 16
crisis services, manic depression 20
Cushing's syndrome and depression 5

dementia 5, 16
depression 1-23
    causes see causes of depression
    and the elderly 22-3
    manic depression 19
    and men 13-15
    and physical illness 2, 5-6
    seeking help 2-3
    self-help 3, 39
    and suicide 10
    treatment see treating depression
    and underage drinking 9
diet

as help for depression 3, 39
    and mental ill-health 11-12
    and SAD 38
dietary trends 11-12
divorce and male depression 14
drug treatment 7, 22, 32, 35
    antidepressants see antidepressants
    manic depression 19
drug use and depression
    ecstasy 10
    prescription drugs 5-6

ecstasy and depression 10
elderly people and depression 22-3
electroconvulsive therapy (ECT) 25-6, 34, 35
emotional disorders, young people 9
endocrine disorders and depression 5
endogenous depression 4
exercise as help for depression 3, 20, 39

family support for manic depressives 20
fatherhood and depression 14
food see diet
friends as support 20

gay men and depression 15
gender and depression 2
genetic disposition to depression 2

healthy eating as help for depression 3, 39
heart disease and depression 5
help for depression 3
    children 28
    men 13, 15
    self-help see self-help
    young people 9
    see also treating depression
hospital admission and manic depression 19-20
hypertension (high blood pressure) and depression
    5

illness and depression 2, 5-6
infections and depression 5

light therapy for seasonal affective disorder 18, 37

mania 19
manic depression 2, 4, 19-20
MDMA (ecstasy) and depression 10
men and depression 13-15
mental health
    and diet 11-12
    statistics 16
monoamine oxidase inhibitors (MAOIs) 32
mood stabilising drugs 19, 25
multiple sclerosis and depression 5

nervous system diseases and depression 5
nutrition *see* diet 39

offending and mental health problems 16
older people
   and depression 22-3
   and mental health problems 16

Parkinson's disease and depression 5
personality susceptibility to depression 2
physical activity as help for depression 3, 20, 39
physical illness and depression 2, 5-6
positive thinking as help for depression 3
postnatal depression 4, 17-18
pregnancy and male depression 14
prescribed drugs and depression 5-6
psychological therapy 7, 26, 33
psychosurgery 26

reactive depression 4
relationships and depression, men 14
relaxation as self-help 39
retirement and male depression 15
risk factors for depression 6

seasonal affective disorder (SAD) 4, 18, 37-8
seeking help for depression 2-3
   men 13-14
selective serotonin re-uptake inhibitors (SSRIs) 8, 10,
   32
self-help 3, 39
   manic depression 20
   postnatal depression 17-18
separation and divorce, and male depression 14
sex and male depression 14
side effects
   anti-depressants 32
   electroconvulsive therapy 34
   SAD treatments 37-8
signs of depression *see* symptoms of depression
social problem of depression 7
social therapies 26
SSRIs (selective serotonin re-uptake inhibitors) 8, 10, 32

St John's wort, treatment for SAD 37-8
statistics on mental health 16
strokes and depression 5
suicide 16
   and depression 10, 22
   men 15
support
   for manic depressives 20
   for postnatal depression 18
symptoms of depression 1, 13
   in the elderly 22-3
   manic depression 19
   postnatal depression 17
   seasonal affective disorder 18
   teenagers 8

talking *see* communication
talking therapies 29-30
   access to 30-31
teenagers *see* young people
treating depression 24-39
   antidepressants *see* antidepressants
   children 27-8
   electroconvulsive therapy 25-6, 34, 35
   elderly people 23
   manic depression 19-20
   postnatal depression 17-18
   psychotherapies 29-31
   seasonal affective disorder 18
   talking therapies 29-31
   young people 8
tricyclics 32

underage drinking and depression 9
unemployment and male depression 14-15
unipolar depression 10

vascular diseases and depression 5
violent men and depression 15

young people
   and depression 8, 9
   and mental health problems 16

ADDITIONAL RESOURCES

Other Issues titles

If you are interested in researching further the issues raised in *Understanding Depression*, you may want to read the following titles in the **Issues** series as they contain additional relevant articles:

- Vol. 123 *Young People and Health* (ISBN 1 86168 362 6)

- Vol. 100 *Stress and Anxiety* (ISBN 1 86168 314 6)

- Vol. 84 *Mental Wellbeing* (ISBN 1 86168 279 4)

For more information about these titles, visit our website at www.independence.co.uk/publicationslist

Useful organisations

You may find the websites of the following organisations useful for further research:

- Depression Alliance: www.depressionalliance.org

- The Manic Depression Fellowship: www.mdf.org.uk

- The Mental Health Foundation: www.mentalhealth.org.uk

- The Royal College of Psychiatrists: www.rcpsych.ac.uk

- The Samaritans: www.samaritans.org.uk

- SANE: www.sane.org.uk

ACKNOWLEDGEMENTS

The publisher is grateful for permission to reproduce the following material.

While every care has been taken to trace and acknowledge copyright, the publisher tenders its apology for any accidental infringement or where copyright has proved untraceable. The publisher would be pleased to come to a suitable arrangement in any such case with the rightful owner.

Chapter One: Depression

Depression, © Royal College of Psychiatrists, *Terms you might hear*, © Depression Alliance, *Depression and physical illness*, © Net Doctor, *Are you at risk for depression?*, © Wing of Madness, *Depression is UK's biggest social problem*, © Guardian Newspapers Ltd, *Teenage depression*, © iVillage UK, *Depression and underage drinking*, © Associated Newspapers Ltd, *Ecstasy and depression*, © TheSite.org, *Depression and suicide*, © The Samaritans, *New reports link mental ill-health to changing diets*, © Mental Health Foundation, *Men and depression*, © Royal College of Psychiatrists, *Statistics on mental health*, © Mental Health Foundation, *Post-natal depression*, © Parentline Plus, *Feeling SAD?*, © TheSite.org, *Manic depression*, © SANE, *Myths and misconceptions about depression*, © World Health Organization, *Depression in the elderly*, © Net Doctor.

Chapter Two: Treating Depression

Treating depression, © Net Doctor, *Pills 'are not best way to treat child depression'*, © Telegraph Group Ltd, *Tips on depression and anxiety in children*, © Parentline Plus, *Introduction to talking therapies*, © Manic Depression Fellowship, *End of the 'prozac nation'*, © Crown copyright is reproduced with the permission of Her Majesty's Stationery Office, *Quick guide to antidepressants*, © SANE, *Psychotherapy for all?*, © Centre for Economic Performance/LSE, *Electroconvulsive therapy*, © TheSite.org, *Responding to depression*, © Guardian Newspapers Ltd, *Cheers?*, © Mental Health Foundation, *The lowdown: seasonal affective disorder (SAD)*, © Guardian Newspapers Ltd, *Quick-fix tips for depression*, © Depression Alliance.

Photographs and illustrations:

Pages 1, 16, 29, 33: Angelo Madrid; pages 3, 25, 32, 36, 39: Simon Kneebone; pages 7, 28: Bev Aisbett; pages 12, 23, 30, 34: Don Hatcher.

Craig Donnellan
Cambridge
September, 2006

South East Essex College
of Arts & Technology
Luker Road Southend-on-Sea Essex SS1 1ND
Tel (01702) 220400 Fax (01702) 432320 Minicom: (01702) 220642